Our Environment

TIME LIFE Student Library

Our Environment

Time-Life Books   Alexandria, Virginia

Table of Contents

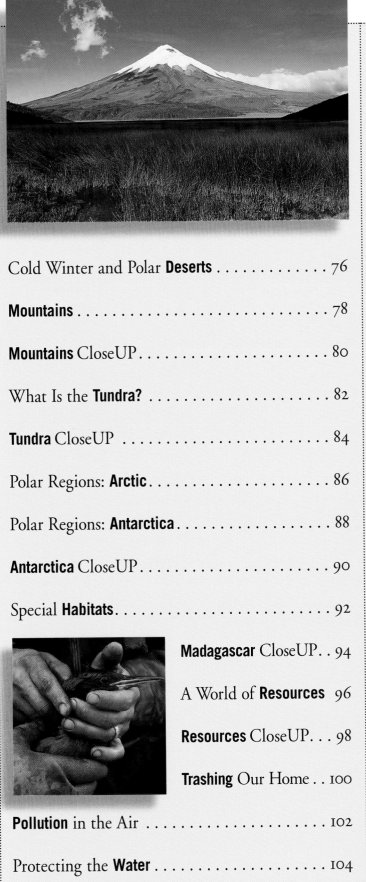

Our Precious Home

Whether you live on a farm, in a small town, or on a big-city street, you are part of an **environment**. You depend on your environment for the air you breathe, the water you drink, and the food you eat. In turn, you affect the world around you in countless ways. The simple act of taking out the garbage can change your environment. Every piece of trash that you don't recycle will be trucked away to a landfill. And those items that are not **biodegradable** will sit there for hundreds of years.

The idea that every action you take has an effect on the world around you is an important part of the science of ecology. Ecology is a Greek word that means "the study of home." Ecologists study the relationships between all living things, as well as their relationship to the nonliving parts of their environment. Their subjects can be as small as a tadpole in the pond at right, or as large as the entire earth. Today humans are drastically altering local and global environments with pollution, overuse of resources, and overpopulation. Ecologists seek to understand and interpret the changes and find safe solutions for the global environment we call home.

Could a single butterfly flapping its wings in South America disturb weather patterns in another part of the world? Ecologists would have a difficult time proving the connection, but it raises an interesting point. Our environment consists of a vast network of links between living and nonliving things. Scientists are certain that even a small change can affect the global environment.

Walden Pond

The writer Henry David Thoreau spent two years in a one-room cabin on Walden Pond *(above)* in northeastern Massachusetts. In 1854, he published his observations about the changing seasons and life in the woods in a book called *Walden*. "In wilderness," he wrote, "is the preservation of the world." Thoreau's work was an early call for human beings to learn to appreciate—and **preserve**—their environment.

Spheres of Life

A thin shell of air, water, and land—called the biosphere—holds all of life on earth. The biosphere measures just 20 km (12 mi.) from top to bottom and contains three very different **environments**. The atmosphere is the air we breathe. It also filters harmful **radiation** from the sun while letting heat and light pass through. The hydrosphere consists of all the water on earth. The water circulates through the entire biosphere in a never-ending cycle. The lithosphere is earth's rocky outer shell, including the continents and the ocean floor. Soil on the surface of the lithosphere supports the growth of plants and trees. Together, these three spheres provide the support system for life on earth.

Exosphere

Thermosphere

Mesosphere

Stratosphere

Troposphere

The Water Cycle

The water in the hydrosphere is constantly in motion *(below)*. The sun evaporates water from the oceans. This water vapor collects in clouds, then falls back to earth as rain. Rivers and streams carry the water back to the ocean.

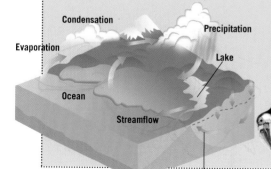

Condensation

Precipitation

Evaporation

Lake

Ocean

Streamflow

Ground Water

Lithosphere

Earth's outer shell is broken into about a dozen large pieces, called tectonic plates, that float over the molten rock below. The plates' movement is slowly rearranging the continents at a rate of about 3 cm (1 in.) per year.

Biosphere

Life abounds in the biosphere *(below)*, thanks to the interaction of land, air, and water. Earth is the only planet known to contain all three of these life-giving spheres.

Air

Cirrus clouds, formed from frozen water vapor high in the atmosphere, are an early sign that storms may be on the way.

Water

More than 97 percent of all the water on earth is held in the world's oceans, whose average depth is 4 km (2.5 mi.).

Land

Soil in the lithosphere plays a vital role in cycling water and other nutrients through the biosphere.

Atmosphere

The atmosphere can be divided into five distinct layers *(left)*. Each layer is thinner in density until it fades away into space about 900 km (560 mi.) above the earth's surface. **Oxygen** and nitrogen make up almost 98 percent.

Biosphere

Life forms can be found in every corner of the biosphere, from Antarctica's frozen ice to steaming hot vents at the bottom of the ocean.

Hydrosphere

Covering about 75 percent of our blue planet, the hydrosphere regulates earth's climate by soaking up heat from the sun and moving it around the globe through ocean currents.

Cycles _{of} Life

The material that makes up your body, and all life on earth, has been around for a long time, constantly cycling through the biosphere. One of the basic laws of science is that matter can neither be created nor destroyed. This means that your molecules may once have been in a tree, a shark, or even a dinosaur! The continuous recycling of materials, combined with a steady flow of energy supplied by the sun, keeps the biosphere healthy.

Six elements make up almost 98 percent of all matter contained in life forms: **oxygen,** carbon, hydrogen, nitrogen, phosphorus, and sulfur. While an organism is alive it takes in new elements by eating, drinking, and breathing and expels old ones in waste products. When an organism dies, it decomposes, releasing its chemical elements back into the biosphere. These recycled elements will then support a new generation of life.

Flower Power

The cycle of life in green plants is called photosynthesis. Sunlight provides the power for the process *(diagram, right).* Plants combine **carbon dioxide** from the air and water from their roots to make glucose, a kind of sugar, which they use to grow. Plants also take up **nutrients** such as nitrogen and phosphorus from the soil. These nutrients then pass into the bodies of animals that feed on the plants, or return to the biosphere when the plant dies. Sunlight is always available to power a new day of growth.

Sun

Carbon dioxide

Water

Sugars and starches

Oxygen produced as a result of photosynthesis

Energy for life

The Nitrogen Cycle

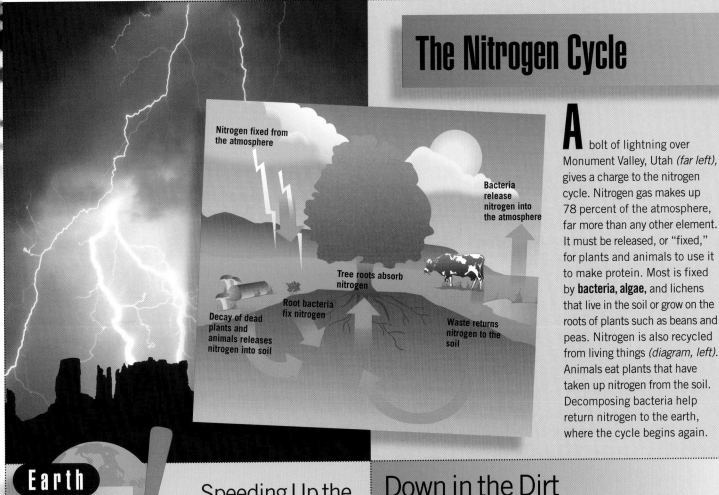

Nitrogen fixed from the atmosphere

Bacteria release nitrogen into the atmosphere

Tree roots absorb nitrogen

Root bacteria fix nitrogen

Decay of dead plants and animals releases nitrogen into soil

Waste returns nitrogen to the soil

A bolt of lightning over Monument Valley, Utah *(far left)*, gives a charge to the nitrogen cycle. Nitrogen gas makes up 78 percent of the atmosphere, far more than any other element. It must be released, or "fixed," for plants and animals to use it to make protein. Most is fixed by **bacteria, algae,** and lichens that live in the soil or grow on the roots of plants such as beans and peas. Nitrogen is also recycled from living things *(diagram, left)*. Animals eat plants that have taken up nitrogen from the soil. Decomposing bacteria help return nitrogen to the earth, where the cycle begins again.

Earth ALERT!

Speeding Up the Carbon Cycle

Unless we cut back on our dependence on oil *(left)* and earth's other **fossil fuels,** these natural energy sources could soon run low. Oil, coal, and natural gas are the remains of ancient carbon cycles. They formed when plants and animals died and were preserved under pressure far beneath the earth's surface. Fossil fuels are used to run everything from electrical power plants to lawn mowers to airplanes. Although a certain amount of the total carbon on earth is circulating in the biosphere, we are using **natural resources** up much faster than nature can replace them through the carbon cycle.

Down in the Dirt

Soil is alive! If you looked at a clump of dirt *(below)* through a powerful magnifying glass, you would see hundreds of earthworms, mites, bacteria, and other organisms. They live among the weathered rocks and decayed plant and animal material that make up soil. Earthworms help to circulate nutrients through the soil. Then the plant roots stretching down from above absorb them and make them available to the rest of the **ecosystem.**

In an Ecosystem

You could learn a lot about an elephant by measuring its trunk, feeling its rough skin, and observing what it ate and where it drank. But you could learn more if you had a whole herd and watched how the elephants behaved with one another for protection, mating, and raising their young. You could discover still more if you saw how they responded to **predators,** interacted with competitors, and coped with life under Africa's sun on the **savanna.**

To get the best information about elephants, you would have to study their entire **ecosystem**—the **community** of animals, plants, and their surroundings. The savanna is an ecosystem; so is a forest, a swamp, or a river. Each of these **environments** supplies the basic materials for life for its particular life forms.

Ecosystems support a complex web of relationships between living creatures and nonliving parts of their environment, including water, minerals, and sunlight. Large ecosystems, such as grasslands, deserts, tundra, and **temperate** forests, are called **biomes.**

INDIVIDUAL

In the photo above, a lone elephant roams the savanna of eastern Africa. An **individual** is the basic unit of an ecosystem, but no living thing can survive entirely on its own. This elephant must find plants to eat, water to drink, and a mate to help it continue the **species.**

POPULATION

A group of animals of the same species is called a **population.** Here a herd of elephants with their young travel through a lake. Elephants live together for protection and to share food resources. Other species, such as tigers and bears, come together only for mating.

COMMUNITY

The combined populations of living things in an ecosystem make up a community. At the watering hole above, antelopes and elephants gather for a drink. The plants growing in the area, even the microorganisms in the soil and water, are part of the community.

Strange But TRUE!

Worlds in a Water Drop

Although an entire lake can be called an ecosystem, so can a muddy puddle on the sidewalk. An ecosystem can be as large as the earth or as small as the drop of water at left. This tiny ecosystem has boundaries that set it apart from the leaf it lies on. Within its walls move billions of **microorganisms,** living together in a community that produces enough **nutrients** for their survival. Another ecosystem is your eyebrow, which is home to tiny mites that feed on flakes of dried skin.

The Big Picture

Elephants, antelopes, and a soaring egret share the watering hole ecosystem at left. This ecosystem is composed of many more animals hidden from view. In fact, every animal, plant, and microorganism in a given area—including its soil, water, air, climate, and amount of available sunlight—helps shape the particular characteristics of an ecosystem.

What's a Niche?

Where an animal lives and what it eats—as well as who eats it—describe the **niche** that it occupies in an ecosystem. No two species occupy exactly the same niche. This limits competition for resources. The weaverbird *(above)* creates its unique place by building woven hanging nests in an attempt to stay out of reach of tree snakes and other **predators.**

Biodiversity

oisonous tree frogs, towering redwoods, and mammoth blue whales all contribute to the variety of life, or **biodiversity.** Scientists have identified more than 1.75 million different species of plants and animals in earth's biosphere. Some estimate that many millions more have yet to be discovered.

Biodiversity is commonly measured by counting the number of species in a given **ecosystem.** Peru's biologically diverse Manu National Park, an area half the size of Luxembourg, is home to more species than in all of North America. Some of them are found nowhere else on earth. Such diversity is valuable for pure scientific knowledge, but it is even more important for its practical uses. Biodiversity has the potential to give us new foods, medicines, and products that haven't even been dreamed of yet. Our own actions can threaten this valuable **natural resource** by destroying precious **habitat** for species and polluting fragile ecosystems.

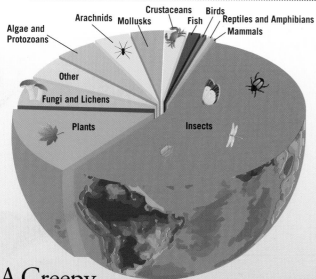

Arachnids
Algae and Protozoans
Mollusks
Crustaceans
Fish
Birds
Reptiles and Amphibians
Mammals
Other
Fungi and Lichens
Plants
Insects

A Creepy-Crawly World

Insects rule the world of living things. They make up more than half of all known species *(above),* even without arachnids, the group that includes spiders, scorpions, mites, and ticks. Plants are the second-largest group, followed by fungi and lichens. Mammals make up less than 1 percent.

The Value of Biodiversity

cientists are looking to nature, in all its diversity, for inspiration in developing new things—everything from a frying pan that resists sticky substances the way a lotus leaf does to a car that will run on tree sap, such as the sap of the copaiba tree. The sticky threads holding a mussel shell *(below)* to a rock may one day help surgeons seal wounds without using stitches.

A treetop observation platform in Costa Rica allows visitors to study one of the most diverse habitats on earth, the rain forest canopy. A year-round growing season and plenty of rain have created forests that hold as many as 300 different kinds of trees per 2.5 sq km (1 sq mi.).

Beetle Mania!

More than one-fifth of all life forms on earth are beetles! The collection below is only a small sampling of the more than 350,000 known species. Their hard outer shell allows beetles to survive in a broad range of habitats. In some species the shell even holds small pockets of air for living underwater.

Who's Watching Whom?

A polar bear greets a bus full of ecotourists in Canada's Churchill Wilderness area. Ecotourists care little for luxury hotels; they travel to learn about the particular nature of different ecosystems, and they try not to disturb nature. In many **endangered** areas, ecotourism has helped local residents realize the value of preserving biodiversity.

People — Carolus Linnaeus

Naming Species

Do you have a *Canis familiaris* or a *Felis catus* in your house? These are the names for dog and cat in the Linnaean system of classification. Back in the 1700s, a Swedish scientist named Carl von Linné set out to find a system for naming all plant and animal species. He wanted scientists in every country to be able to understand it. In the system he invented, two Latin words are used to identify a **species,** the first to name its

genus, the second to name the species. Linné even changed his own name to Latin as Carolus Linnaeus. He thought that sounded more scientific!

The Food Chain

A dragonfly that feeds on nectar-drinking butterflies is caught by the quick tongue of a yellow-bellied toad.

Energy and matter pass from one living thing to another in the biosphere through food chains. Most food chains begin with the sun, whose energy allows plants to grow by using photosynthesis. Because they can make their own food, plants are called producers. Organisms that depend on other living things for their food are called consumers. Herbivores are animals that rely solely on plants for their food, whereas carnivores feed on the flesh of herbivores and other carnivores.

Each separate stage of feeding in a food chain is called a trophic level. As energy moves up the chain from one trophic level to another, most of it is used by the organism to live, or is lost to the biosphere as heat. Only about 10 percent is passed on to the next trophic level. As a result, food chains require a great many producers to support a smaller number of consumers further along the chain.

Camouflaged by leaf litter on the forest floor, a snake swallows an unfortunate frog. Most snakes eat only one large **prey** per meal, taking days to digest the bounty.

Earth ALERT!

Passing Along Poison

DDT was a powerful chemical **pesticide** used in the 1940s. It was passed up the food chain from **microorganisms** in the water to fish and then to fish-eating birds. Peregrine falcons' eggshells became so weak as a result of concentrated poison that scientists placed lab-grown eggs *(right)* in wild nests to save the species from extinction.

An eagle chick eagerly awaits a snake dinner caught by its parent. The sharp eyes of these carnivorous birds can spot prey hiding in a field or **forest** from high up in the air.

Who's Who in the Food Chain

Producers
Producers use sunlight, nitrogen, and **carbon dioxide** to make starches and proteins.

Carnivores
Carnivores feed on the flesh of herbivores and sometimes on other carnivores.

Scavengers
Scavengers feed on the bodies of dead animals, which are called carrion.

Herbivores
Herbivores get their energy from **nutrients** stored in the green plants they eat.

Omnivores
Omnivores eat both plants and animals. Most human beings are omnivores.

Decomposers
Decomposers break down dead organisms into simple chemical elements.

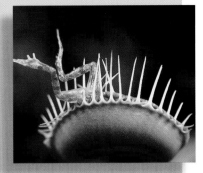
Food Web

An **ecosystem** is made up of a network of food chains, called a food web. Most animals depend on more than one kind of food for survival. In turn, most of them are pursued by more than one type of **predator**. The crayfish, for example, is a food source for the blue heron, the raccoon, and the fish. The heron and the raccoon may be food for the alligator.

Pyramid of Energy

This pyramid shows how energy is lost in a food chain as it moves from one trophic level to the next. More energy is needed at the lower trophic levels to support higher ones. Many plants must be consumed by herbivores to in turn feed the carnivores so that those at the top of the pyramid (including humans) will survive.

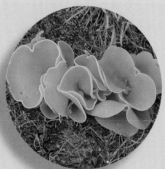

Top Carnivore (Owl)

Carnivore (Shrew)

Herbivore (Beetle)

Green Plant

The Struggle to Survive

Staying alive is no easy task. Every day, plants and animals must contend with a variety of dangers in their **environments** and threats from other **species.** Most animals must stay ever alert to the presence of **predators.** One brief slip of attention could be fatal.

Predators are usually larger and stronger than their **prey.** But the victims do not just lie around waiting to be eaten. Prey species have developed many ways to defend themselves and escape their enemies. Some animals run quickly and live in groups for protection. Others are colored to blend in with their surroundings, and some simply play dead when danger looms.

To make the struggle for survival even tougher, members of the same species often fight with one another for food and space. Trees in the **forest,** for example, compete for available sunlight and **nutrients** from the soil. And animals frequently clash over territory and mates.

Safety in Numbers
Sensing danger, a herd of impalas bound away in many directions. Highly developed senses of sight, smell, and hearing help this species survive in a hazardous environment.

Big Bluffer
When threatened, the Australian frilled lizard hisses, thrashes its tail, and opens the flaps on either side of its head. This makes the lizard look much larger and thus more frightening to predators.

Strange! But TRUE

Plant Protection

Thorns and prickers are one way for plants to prevent animals from nibbling, but some plants use chemical warfare to protect themselves. Peppermint, cinnamon, and the mustard plant—from which mustard powder is ground—all contain strongly flavored chemicals that animals find unpleasant but that taste delicious to humans.

Blending In
Special coloring and texture, called **camouflage,** help this leaf insect blend in with its surroundings in the Malaysian jungle. To complete the disguise, it must remain still when predators are near.

Predation

Sprinting at speeds up to 110 km/h (70 mph), a cheetah closes in on a gazelle. The cheetah is a fearsome hunter, but like all predators, it depends on the prey in its environment to provide energy for its survival. If drought or poaching reduces the herds of gazelles and other cheetah food, **populations** of these mighty cats shrink as well.

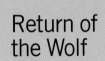

Warts and Snorts

Two male African warthogs *(right)* grapple in a battle over a prospective mate. Competition between members of the same species is common when issues of mating or group dominance are at stake. Four wartlike growths on the face of this homely hog help protect it from the sharp tusks of other suitors during such battles.

Return of the Wolf

Once seen as a threat to elk and deer within Yellowstone National Park— as well as to nearby live-stock—wolves in the park were hunted to extinction by 1950. When this predator was removed, populations of the wolves' prey soared beyond the limits of available food, and many animals starved to death. In 1995, scientists reintroduced wolves to the park, where it is hoped they will help restore the natural balance of predator and prey in this **ecosystem.**

Getting Along

Not every relationship in nature is competitive. A surprising number of **species** have found ways to get along. They provide protection from **predators,** keep one another clean, or provide food for one another. The partnerships between different species of plants or animals are called **symbiosis,** which means "living together."

Symbiosis takes many forms: **Mutualism** benefits both species. Ants, for example, protect tiny aphids from predators and in turn milk the aphids for a sugary juice called nectar. **Commensalism** occurs when one species benefits and the other is neither harmed nor helped, such as when a raccoon raids a human's trash can, or a remora swims with a shark for protection from other fish and the chance for leftover food scraps. When one species lives off another and causes it some harm, it is engaging in parasitism.

Fine-Feathered Friends

The Clark's nutcracker *(above)* and the red-billed oxpecker *(below)* have formed strong mutualistic relations with their "partners." Nutcrackers help whitebark pines reproduce by cracking the tough cones and releasing the seeds. Oxpeckers keep the Cape buffalo pest free.

Mutualistic arrangements usually occur between species with widely differing needs. The Clark's nutcracker *(left)* thrives on the seeds of the whitebark pine, but the pine cones do not open on their own. With the help of the nutcracker's sharp beak, the seeds are released. Seeds that the bird drops or buries for winter storage and then forgets will sprout to become new pine trees. In a similar search for a never-ending food supply, the oxpecker picks off ticks and bloodsucking flies from the Cape buffalo's ears and nose, relieving the buffalo of pesky intruders.

Hitching a Ride

Without legs, arms, or wings, barnacles are still champion long-distance travelers. They can wander as far as 20,000 km (12,000 mi.) a year by attaching themselves to the hulls of ships or the skin of **marine** animals such as turtles and humpback whales *(right)*. Barnacles feed on microscopic plankton in the water. Their commensal relationship with whales exposes them to an ever changing undersea buffet. A single whale may carry as much as 0.4 t (0.5 tn.) of these tiny "hitchhikers."

The Lure of Rotting Meat

The tempting aroma of rotting meat draws pollinating flies to the giant rafflesia plant in Southeast Asia. The rafflesia is a parasite that can grow as large as the wheel of a truck. Its roots tap nutrients from the stems and roots of vines that grow along the forest floor.

Strange But TRUE!

What's a Parasite?

Bloodsucking ticks *(right)* are **parasites**—species that take their nutrition from a **host** and give nothing back. Although a parasite steals **nutrients,** it seldom takes enough to kill the host. Doing so would cost it a steady source of food. Mistletoe *(right)* is a plant parasite. It grows in ball-shaped clumps in the branches of trees, putting roots into the tree to divert some of its nutrients. Because it stays evergreen and appears to grow with no roots at all, people once believed that mistletoe possessed magical powers to repel witches and cure toothaches.

Osprey Landlords

Ospreys build massive nests in treetops and on utility poles, often returning year after year to the same home. Just below their large nests some smaller birds like to seek shelter. Herons, grackles, wrens, and sparrows have been known to build their own nests below, benefiting from the sharp eyes and protection of the fish-eating shorebird. The osprey is neither harmed nor helped by this commensal relationship, but it doesn't seem to mind the presence of these smaller tenants even though they sometimes raid the larger nest for leftover food scraps.

Adapting to the Environment

Everywhere you look in nature, plants and animals seem to have adapted to fit perfectly into their **environment.** Wings and feathers make flying a breeze for birds. Echolocation, which works sort of like radar, allows bats to navigate and hunt at night. Layers of insulating blubber and thick fur enable polar bears to survive long winters in the freezing Arctic.

Adaptation happens as **species** respond to changes in their environment. Through **natural selection,** species with features that are well suited to their environment survive and pass their **genes** on to the next generation. Over long periods of time, changes brought about through natural selection can create new and more biologically complex species. This is the natural process of **evolution.**

Stretching high for a snack, a giraffe nibbles on acacia leaves. Over millions of years, the giraffe has evolved a long neck to take advantage of this favorite food. Acacias may also have adapted to the giraffe by growing taller to make sure at least some of their leaves survive the constant grazing.

Let's Compare Snow Bunnies, Beach Bunnies

Arctic Hare

Desert Jack Rabbit

Huddled against the cold, the arctic hare *(left top)* is well equipped for the cold climate in its polar environment. The hare's short ears and legs and large body help it **conserve** as much heat as possible during cold winter months. In contrast, the very long ears of the jack rabbit *(left bottom)* help beat the heat in the desert where it lives. Heat is drawn away from its body over the large surface area of the ears and through its long legs. The coloring of both species blends in with their environment. The jack rabbit stays the color of desert sand year round, and the hare turns white in winter to match the snow.

Adapting to Cold and Heat

Baobab Tree

Baobab trees look like they were planted upside down, but their shape actually helps them conserve water in the **arid** climates of Africa, India, and Australia. Baobabs lose little water through their sparse leaves and branches and can store as much as two backyard swimming pools' worth of water in their fat trunks. Superb survivors, baobabs can live for more than 3,000 years.

Moss Campion

Fierce winds and freezing temperatures are constant threats to pink-budded moss campion, which grows on the Arctic tundra. In response to these harsh conditions, the plant sprouts in small, tightly packed clumps close to the ground. Inside the clump, temperatures can be as much as several degrees warmer than the surrounding air.

People — Charles Darwin

Large Tree Finch

Large Ground Finch

Sharp-Beaked Finch

Woodpecker Finch

While in the Galápagos Islands off the coast of South America in 1835, Charles Darwin observed 13 different species of finch, each with a beak that was adapted to the food it ate. He theorized that the birds had evolved from one species, changing to take advantage of different foods. Darwin's theory of evolution is based on such observations.

Dead As a Dodo?

Earth ALERT!

Extinction, the disappearance of a species, is a natural part of evolution. But sometimes one species' extinction can have a critical effect on others. The last dodo bird *(right)* was killed 300 years ago, but in 1973 an ecologist discovered that the **endangered** *Calvaria major* tree was in desperate trouble. No new trees had grown in the last 300 years because nuts from the tree needed to pass through the intestines of the dodo, where their hard shells were broken down. The tree was saved when the nuts were fed to turkeys, which have similar intestines.

What Is Climate?

The ecology of a region is influenced by its climate—the combined temperature, **precipitation,** and wind conditions that usually exist. Rain forests flourish in the moist, warm climate near the **equator,** for example, but only a few hardy plants and animals make their homes in the dry, frigid polar climate.

Climate is caused by a complex interplay of wind, water, and land. Sunlight warms the earth and its atmosphere, creating rising and falling columns of air. Together with the earth's rotation, these columns of air generate atmospheric currents. The air currents help generate ocean currents, which carry warm or cold water all around the world.

It is important to remember that climate is not the same as weather. Climate refers to large-scale atmospheric conditions of an area, averaged over many years, and weather to what the atmospheric conditions are like in a specific place at a specific time: if it's raining in London today, or if it snowed in Chicago last Wednesday, for example.

Land, Sea, and Atmosphere

A satellite photo shows earth's atmosphere churning from the force of a hurricane. The swirling clouds are the result of energy transferred from the sun to the oceans, and into the atmosphere. Some hurricanes contain as much energy as the United States consumes in a week.

Climates around the World

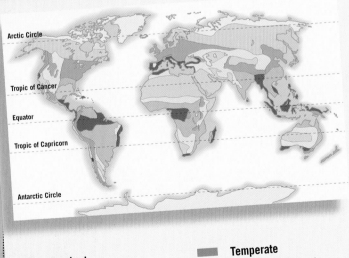

- Arctic Circle
- Tropic of Cancer
- Equator
- Tropic of Capricorn
- Antarctic Circle

- Tropical
- Subtropical
- Arid
- Semiarid
- Mediterranean
- Temperate
- Northern Temperate
- Mountain
- Polar
- Coastal

Motion of Wind and Water

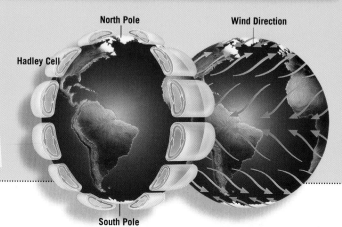

North Pole

Wind Direction

Hadley Cell

South Pole

The Four Seasons

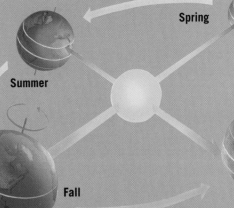

Seasons change because the earth is tilted on its axis in its orbit around the sun. When the northern half of the globe is tilted toward the sun, the land heats up, and it is summer there. When this hemisphere is tilted away from the sun, the land receives less sunlight. Then the air turns cold, and it is winter.

Let's Compare

Air heated by sunlight warms and rises, then cools and falls to form patterns called Hadley cells, as shown on the globe at far left. The west-to-east rotation of the earth then twists these cells into global winds, as seen in the globe at near left. These wind patterns sweep ocean water into currents that circulate water around the world. The maps at upper left show warm-water currents in red and cold-water movements in blue. Deserts often form where cold water and dry air meet land, whereas rain forests with lush vegetation flourish where warm water and moist air meet land.

Desert

Rain Forest

Winter

Summer

Winter snows and summer greenery illustrate the change of seasons. In the Southern Hemisphere, summer comes in December and winter in June, whereas in the Northern Hemisphere, it's the reverse.

How Climate Changes

Climates can change over short or long periods of time. For most of the earth's 4.6-billion-year history, it has been much warmer than it is today. During only seven periods has the planet been cold enough to have large ice formations on its surface. (The most recent ice age has not yet ended.) At the time of these ice ages temperatures deviated from warmer "interglacial periods" like today's to colder periods in which much of the world was covered in thick sheets of ice. The last full-fledged ice age peaked about 18,000 years ago, though ice sheets still covererd parts of what would become the U.S. just 10,000 years ago.

Scientists use complex methods to find out how climate has changed over such long periods. Smaller, more sudden changes over just a few years can be measured easily. The effects of volcanic eruptions are one example, as is the atmospheric phenomenon known as El Niño.

Would You Believe?

The "Little Ice Age"

Big chunks of ice cover the Thames River in London, England, in this 1677 painting. Photography was not yet invented, so art served to report on the "little ice age," when the river froze 10 times. The river never freezes today.
In addition to recent ice ages, there have been numerous less drastic cold periods through-out history.

Climate Changes

The Mysterious El Niño

The rain-filled Sechura Desert in Peru *(below)* is normally one of the driest places on earth. But every two to seven years, ocean currents reverse their course. This creates an unusual climate change called El Niño. One result is that the desert suddenly receives a lot of rain.

March of the Ice

Aglacier forms a frozen cascade in Alaska. **Glaciers** were a common sight during earth's last ice age, some 18,000 years ago. The inset map shows in blue the parts of the earth covered in ice at that time. Green represents the shapes of the continents then. They were larger than today, because all the ice lowered sea levels by about 120 m (400 ft.).

Volcanic Dust

Ash clouds released by the 1991 eruption of Mount Pinatubo in the Philippines *(right)* quickly spread around the world *(dark green on map)*. The dust blocked enough sunlight to cause a global temperature drop of one degree.

Monitoring Climate Change

CORE SAMPLES

The geologists at left drill deep into the ice in Antarctica to obtain a long cylinder of ice. Air bubbles trapped in the ice provide clues as to what the climate was like when the ice formed. The deeper the ice, the further back in time the ice formed. These samples allow scientists to figure out what climates were like as much as 160,000 years ago. The study of core samples around the world provides a record of how climates have changed.

POLLEN GRAINS

Scientists find traces of pollen, such as the hibiscus pollen above (enlarged 100 times), in soil samples drilled from deep lake beds. By analyzing the soil, they can tell what types of plants lived there millennia ago and which climate would have supported the plants.

REMOTE IMAGING

Radar images from the space shuttle reveal amazing changes in earth's climate. The center section in the photo shows ancient riverbeds lying underneath the sands of Africa's Sahara. This is proof that the desert was once wet.

The Ever-Warming Earth

Although it's a good thing that the earth is now much warmer than it was 10,000 years ago, scientists are worried that the planet may be getting too hot. The problem is called global warming, and most experts agree that it may be dangerous. The cause is an atmospheric phenomenon called the greenhouse effect. When sunlight strikes the earth it heats the ground, which then gives off waves of heat energy. When much of this energy is absorbed by the atmosphere, the heat is bounced back to earth, making it warmer. Pollution in the atmosphere—gases such as **carbon dioxide,** methane, and nitrogen compounds—keeps the heat in. About 4.5 billion t (5 billion tn.) of these gases are released into the atmosphere from the burning of coal, oil, and gas every year, increasing the greenhouse effect.

The Greenhouse Effect

The earth is warmed by the sun's rays, which pass through the atmosphere easily. But when the earth radiates heat outward, some of it is absorbed by the greenhouse gases in the earth's atmosphere. The heat becomes trapped and increases the temperature. The more greenhouse gases in the atmosphere, the stronger the effect.

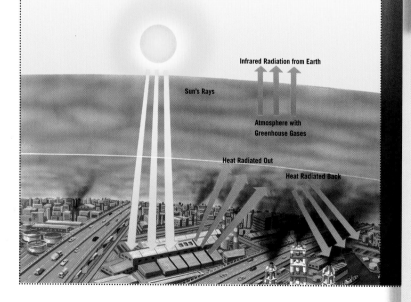

Infrared Radiation from Earth

Sun's Rays

Atmosphere with
Greenhouse Gases

Heat Radiated Out

Heat Radiated Back

Pollution

Smoke and haze hang heavy over the Brazilian city of São Paulo. This type of air pollution contains greenhouse gases like carbon dioxide and nitrogen compounds that absorb the **radiation** of heat from the earth. Many countries have only recently understood this growing problem and are taking steps to reduce the pollution they create. One way to help is by making cars more fuel efficient.

A Hot Time in a Hothouse

The sun's rays radiate through the glass in a greenhouse to warm the plants beneath. As the heat rises to the glass ceiling again, it cannot escape and the heat builds up. The so-called greenhouse gases have a similar blocking effect on earth. The industrialized world—including the U.S., Europe, and Asia—produces three-quarters of these damaging emissions.

The Perils of Melting Ice

One danger of global warming is that rising temperatures will melt much of the ice at the earth's Poles. This will raise sea levels around the world and flood coastal cities. Ice reflects a lot of sunlight into space, which adds to the problem. The more the ice melts, the more heat the earth absorbs, speeding up global warming.

Projecting the Future

The map shows the rise of global temperatures by 2060 if atmospheric greenhouse gases double from current levels. The continents will get warmer by 2°C (3.5°F) and the polar regions by 5°C (9°F).

Annual Mean Temperature Change by 2060

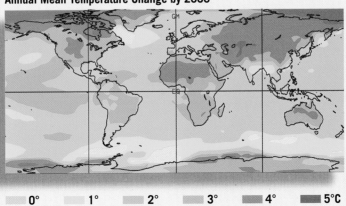

| 0° | 1° | 2° | 3° | 4° | 5°C |

A Runaway Greenhouse

The planet Venus is an example of a rampant greenhouse effect. Many of the gases in Venus's atmosphere—mainly carbon dioxide and sulfuric acid—have created such a strong greenhouse effect that astronomers estimate the planet's average surface temperature at more than 480°C (900°F).

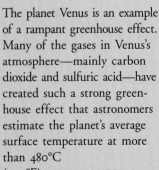

Forests Green Wonders

Woods Lovely, Dark, and Deep

From the freezing Siberian taiga to the hot, steamy rain forests of Africa, **forests** blanket large portions of the earth in canopies of green. They are home to millions of **species** of plants, insects, and animals. Forests also provide wood for building lumber, fuel for fire, and pulp for newspapers and books, as well as **oxygen** for the air we breathe.

Climate and geography determine what type of forest will grow in a particular region. In northern forests, coniferous trees mature slowly and survive the long, cold winters by staying green all year. Farther south, trees grow during spring and summer, then shed their leaves and "sleep" through the winter. The wet, tropical climate near the **equator** lets trees grow year round and reach towering heights. Forests are much more than a collection of trees; they are complex **ecosystems** in which each member of the **community** plays a vital role in continuing the cycle of life.

Where in the World?

Forests

TEMPERATE

Temperate forests change from green to shades of red, yellow, and orange in the fall as **deciduous** trees prepare to drop their leaves. These forests dominate Europe and the eastern United States.

CONIFEROUS

Forests of evergreen, or coniferous, trees are found in northern climates in Asia, Europe, and North America, as well as at high altitudes in mountains farther south.

Fast FACTS

Tallest Tree A coastal redwood in Redwood National Park, California, is 112 m (365 ft.) tall.

Smallest Tree Carefully pruned bonsai, or miniature trees, rarely top 0.3 m (1 ft.).

Thirsty Trees A large tree absorbs as much as 360 l (95 gal.) of water from the soil each day. Water moves at a speed of about 0.9 m (3 ft.) per minute up through the trunk.

Wettest Forest The tropical rain forest in Tytenudo, Colombia, receives almost 12 m (39 ft.) of rainfall per year.

Most Massive Tree General Sherman, a giant sequoia, has a circumference of 25 m (82 ft.) and stands 84 m (275 ft.) tall.

Largest Forest Coniferous taiga of Siberia covers 1.1 billion ha (2.7 billion acres), or 25 percent of the world's forestland.

Conservation

At the urging of John Muir and other concerned Americans, Congress established Yosemite as the second national park in 1890. At left, Muir stands with President Theodore Roosevelt during a 1903 camping trip in Yosemite. Since then, many other nations have created national parks to **conserve** forests and other wild spaces.

Ancient Forest

A grove of giant fern trees in Costa Rica recalls earth's first forests, which appeared more than 350 million years ago, long before the dinosaurs. These earliest trees produced spores that grew into new trees in the tropical climate. Seeds, which allowed plants to develop in harsher conditions, did not evolve until later.

How **Old?**

Bristlecone Pine

Older than the great pyramids of Egypt, bristlecone pine trees are the oldest living things on earth. Rarely more than 8 m (25 ft.) tall, gnarled bristlecones are found at high altitudes in the American West. The oldest known specimen is more than 4,600 years old.

Boreal Forests

Named for Boreas, the Greek god of the north wind, boreal **forests** rival deserts as the earth's largest land-based **biome.** Frigid winters with little sunlight and short summers characterize boreal forests. They are found in the northern regions of North America, Europe, and Asia.

Coniferous trees dominate boreal forests, which are also known by the Russian name taiga. Waxy needle-shaped leaves help them **conserve** moisture through the long winters when **precipitation** and surface water are locked up in snow and ice.

Even during the long season of cold and darkness, the boreal forest is alive. Shrews, voles, and mice scurry through tunnels beneath the snow, which acts as a thick layer of insulation and conceals them from **predators.** Summer brings migratory birds that nest in the trees and feed on insects hatched in the lakes and bogs created by melting snow. Deer, moose, bears, wolves, and wolverines also call these forests home.

Moose on the Loose!

Would You Believe?

Disguised environmentalists Joel Berger and Carol Cunningham *(left)* throw wolf urine-scented snowballs and play taped wolf howls among moose herds to check their reaction. Some run away, but those who live where wolves have been removed from the habitat show no fear.

Earth ALERT !

Fewer than 400 Siberian tigers still roam the taiga of eastern Asia—and they are constantly threatened by **poachers** and loss of **habitat** from logging. Siberian tigers are the largest **species** of cat, weighing up to 300 kg (650 lb.). Their organs and bones are highly valued in traditional medicines, making the lure of poaching irresistible to many poor local residents. Scientists and zoos around the world are helping to **preserve** the remaining **population** and habitat of these magnificent cats.

Needles and Cones

Dark green needles angled in many directions help conifers absorb as much sunlight as possible for photosynthesis during the short summer season. The trees produce seeds in tough, woody cones that stay closed until they are mature. In some species of conifer, the cones open only in the heat of a forest fire.

In warm weather, moose wade into the lakes and ponds of the taiga to feed on aquatic plants. They can eat up to 27 kg (60 lb.) of vegetation in a single day. Moose have been known to submerge their huge bodies completely to escape the millions of mosquitoes and flies that torment forest-dwelling animals during the short summers.

Jurassic Wasp

When a pine tree's branches are cut or broken off, sticky resin oozes out to protect the tree from wood-eating insects. More than 40 million years ago, the wasps above were trapped and smothered in such an ooze. The resin hardened, then over time fossilized and became amber, a glasslike material with a golden color. Amber has preserved feathers, flowers, frogs, and pollen from long ago, but unlike the actors in the movie *Jurassic Park,* scientists have not yet recovered enough DNA to bring long-**extinct** species back to life.

Not Always Evergreen

Larches are **deciduous** conifers that light up the autumn landscape with their golden hue. The hardiest of all conifers, larches shed their leaves in winter to survive damage from frost and drought. Their roots spread out over large areas to absorb moisture and anchor them against winter storms.

Snow Cones

Snow does little damage to the hardy boughs of a conifer. Its conical shape, with the point at the top and a broad base along the ground, allows the tree to support a great deal of snow without breaking. Snow helps insulate conifers against the cold and blocks out sun and wind, which can dry out the tree's needles and branches.

Temperate Deciduous Forests

Stately oaks, maples, and other broad-leaved hardwood trees dominate temperate **forests. Temperate** means not too hot and not too cold, and these forests receive plentiful rain and enjoy a five- to six-month growing season. Temperate forests are constantly changing: **Deciduous** trees are fresh with green leaves in the spring and summer. To prepare for winter they shed their leaves, which fall in autumn to form a thick layer of **nutrient**-rich compost. Last year's leaves fertilize next year's growth when life returns to the forest in the spring.

Humans have dramatically altered the look of temperate forests by logging, clearing land for agriculture, and introducing **pollutants** and foreign **species.** Some of the most densely populated places on earth occupy land where temperate forests once grew. Only scattered traces of the original forests remain.

Earth ALERT!

Back in the Wild

The last wild European bison was killed by a **poacher** in 1921, but a few animals survived in zoos. Careful breeding of those captive bison led to the 1956 release of a small herd in Poland's Bialowieza National Park. Today, more than 500 bison roam there, enough to give hope that the species will survive on its own.

The Forest Takes Over

Early settlers cleared acres of forest in New England for farming. They built sturdy walls with the rocks removed from the soil. Many farms were later abandoned, and the forest crept back, leaving only the stone walls to mark the boundaries of long-ago fields.

What Is Fall?

During the growing season, leaves of deciduous trees give off an enormous amount of water into the air. Shedding leaves allows trees to **conserve** water during the winter, when it may not be available from the ground. As the autumn days grow cooler, the flow of nutrients and water to the leaves slows down. Soft cells, called the separation layer, form around the base of each leaf's stem and stop the flow of sugar made during photosynthesis. The chlorophyll that gave the leaf its green color fades, and the sugar that remains trapped in the leaf causes it to change color. The varied and brilliant hues of fall are based on the makeup of each particular tree. Eventually the separation layer dissolves the base of the stem, and the leaf falls to the ground.

Winter's Sweet Treat

Have you ever wondered where the maple syrup on your pancakes comes from? In the late winter and early spring, a sugary sap flows through the trunks of two different kinds of maple trees found in the eastern United States and Canada. The trees are tapped by having spouts inserted into their trunks so the sap can be collected in buckets.

The sap must be boiled for many hours to evaporate the water it contains. At least 114 l (30 gal.) of sap are needed to make 4 l (1 gal.) of maple syrup.

Fire in the Forest

With parachute billowing, a smokejumper descends into a fire in the Alaskan interior to fight a forest fire. Healthy forests depend on occasional fires to clear undergrowth and rejuvenate the soil. Wild animals usually escape forest blazes. Birds can fly away, and other animals flee at the first whiff of smoke. Some animals wait out the blaze in ponds or streams, whereas others retreat to underground burrows.

Royal Hunt

During the Middle Ages, European royalty discovered that too much hunting was reducing the numbers of deer and wild boar. They set aside large areas of forest as private preserves, where the hunts were carefully controlled.

Forests Close up

Among the branches, inside the trunk, and under the leaves of a single oak tree *(right)* lies an entire forest **ecosystem.** Squirrels make nests, called dreys, between sturdy limbs using leaves and twigs. Woodpeckers use their sharp beaks to drill nest holes and probe behind the bark for insects to eat. As many as 400,000 caterpillars per tree chew the oak's leaves to tatters. In time the caterpillars will become moths and butterflies—if they aren't eaten by small birds first. Nut weevils also feed on oak leaves and use their pointed snouts to bore holes in acorns, where they lay eggs.

Beneath the oak, deer browse on tender shoots of new plants in the summer, or forage for fallen acorns in autumn and winter. Mice and other small mammals stay well hidden on the **forest** floor, ever wary of the sharp-eyed great horned owl and other birds of prey. Mushrooms and other fungi growing at the tree's base help the roots absorb water and minerals. With **bacteria** and insects, fungi break down fallen leaves into elements for new growth.

How Old? History in a Tree

Trees carry a detailed record of the past in their rings. Years of plentiful rain produce wide rings, whereas drought makes them narrow. Dark rings, which separate a tree's springtime growth spurts, are formed in summer and autumn, when the tree does not grow as quickly. The rings below document more than 1,700 years of weather patterns in a forest.

1917 Tree falls—1,710 years old
1914 Start of World War I
1789 French Revolution
1618 Start of 30 Years' War
1580 Drake circumnavigates the globe
1492 Columbus discovers America
1215 Magna Carta signed
1095 First Crusade
800 Coronation of Charlemagne
636 Jerusalem taken by Saracens
449 Saxons invade England

207 Tree begins to grow

CATERPILLAR

DEER

WOODPECKER

OWL

SQUIRREL

Acorn to Tree

Acorns provide a protective shell for an oak tree's seeds. They drop to the ground in early autumn. Then the oak sheds its leaves, which accumulate on top of the acorns, insulating them from cold and concealing some from foraging animals. Only one in about one million acorns will grow into a new tree. Many new oaks sprout from forgotten stashes of acorns stored for the winter by squirrels and birds.

MUSHROOMS

Temperate rain forests are the rarest type of woodlands on earth, covering just 0.02 percent of the land. Sandwiched between high mountains and the ocean in small patches of North and South America, New Zealand, and parts of northern Europe, **temperate** rain forests receive more than 2.5 m (8 ft.) of rain per year on average. In addition, fog can contribute significant amounts of water to the **ecosystem.** These lush sanctuaries of emerald green produce more living material, or biomass, per acre than any other **habitat** on earth.

In North America's Pacific Northwest, home to about half of the world's temperate rain forests, Sitka spruce and western red cedar trees grow to heights of more than 60 m (200 ft.) and have an average life span of 500 to 1,000 years. Redwoods live even longer, some more than 2,000 years. These ancient forests are the sole habitats of many **endangered** species, including the spotted owl.

Strange But TRUE!

Spirit Bear

Kermode bears *(right)* are a rare subspecies of black bear that live in secluded **forests** on islands off the west coast of Canada. A recessive **gene** causes about one in 10 to be born pure white. Others can be tan or spotted with patches of black and white. Native peoples call them moksgum'ol, or spirit bears, and believe they possess great powers.

Roots in the Sky

Ecologist Nalini Nadkarnia clutches a tangle of roots growing straight from the trunk of this big-leaf maple into a small pocket of soil. Beneath the moss lies a fertile layer of decayed plant material, much richer than the soil of the forest floor.

Nurse Log: A Giving Tree

A colonnade of trees straddle a decaying log in Washington State's Hoh rain forest. These "nurse logs" provide **nutrients,** open space, and plenty of light for seedlings above the **undergrowth.**

Tumbling waters from the White Chuck River break up the dense green blanket of ancient conifers and mossy undergrowth in Washington State's Snoqualmie National Forest.

Native Carvers

A yellow cedar from the Hoh rain forest becomes a totem pole under the skilled hands of a Native American carver. In years past, native carvers crafted dugout canoes from these trees that were large enough to hold 30 people.

Then & NOW!

Logging

Forest Giants

The largest trees in the temperate rain forest, like the sequoia above, provide enough lumber to build 80 five-room houses. In the 19th and early 20th centuries, logging companies regularly harvested these giant trees.

Saving Ancient Forests

Today, most of the magnificent sequoias are gone, and many people are fighting to **conserve** those that remain. Areas in which all the trees have been cut down may never recover the wildlife and spectacular beauty of their original state.

Tropical Rain Forests

Tropical rain forests are found in the hot, humid climates that lie near the earth's **equator.** These rain forests cover only 6 percent of earth's land, but they account for far more than half of all **biodiversity.**

The **habitats** in the rain forest are divided into several vertical layers. A dark green canopy of treetops absorbs sunlight, traps moisture, and shelters the **forest** from wind. Most rain forest animals, including birds, insects, frogs, and monkeys, live in the canopy. The emergent layer consists of taller trees that break through the canopy. Their topmost branches, or crowns, may experience near-drought conditions.

Beneath the canopy is the dark, still world of the understory. Here saplings wait for a space to clear in the canopy so that they may take advantage of the sunlight to grow. There are few plants on the rain forest floor, except where light filters through. **Nutrients** are recycled quickly; otherwise they will wash away in the heavy rains. Despite the richness of the rain forest, it is a very fragile **environment.** Land cleared for agriculture will take many hundreds of years to recover as a forest, if it recovers at all.

Frogs in Flowers

Tank **bromeliads** *(right)* take root high on tree trunks and large branches. Their spiky leaves form a watertight pool that collects water, which becomes a miniature **ecosystem.** Lizards, snails, mice, and worms all visit these treetop watering holes. Mosquitoes and frogs use the pools as a breeding ground.

The Arms of a Strangler

Strangler figs creep down from the rain forest canopy, encircling trees in a deadly embrace. The fig gets its moisture and nutrients from the air and the tree. As the fig grows, it slows the flow of water and nutrients to its host. In time the tree dies and rots away, leaving a hollow column of vines *(inset).*

Outdoor Classroom

Saving the Rain Forest

Students get soaked as they learn about the Monteverde Cloud Forest in Costa Rica. Donations from kids in 22 countries helped establish the adjoining Children's Eternal Rain Forest, where more than 15,000 ha (40,000 acres) have been preserved since 1989.

Nature's Pharmacy

Paul Cox dangles from a tree to collect plant samples that might yield new medicines. He is an ethnobotanist, meaning he studies the plant lore of native peoples. By speaking with local healers, he has already located one plant that might help slow the AIDS virus. About 25 percent of all medicines come from rain forest plants, but to date, only about 1 percent of these plants have been studied for their healing abilities.

Forest People

Hunters gather by a waterfall in Papua New Guinea before a bird hunt. Large mammals are rare here, and birds provide a major portion of the people's diet. Their colorful feathers are worn for decoration.

Bright blue plumage crowns the head of the black palm cockatoo above. These rare birds are natives of Indonesia and are among the most vocal animals in the forest. They can mimic the sound of a tiger or the swish of wind passing through the trees.

Orange feet are another distinctive feature of the aptly named red-eyed tree frog. It lives in the Costa Rican rain forest canopy. Suction cups on its toes help it stick to slippery trees.

Mediterranean Forests

In South Africa, these **forests** are called fynbos, in California, chaparral. In Australia they are mallee, and in parts of Europe maquis, matorral, or garrigue. Each name describes the dense shrubs and small trees that grow in Mediterranean climates, which receive just enough rainfall to support a minimal forest. Though they are found on every continent except Antarctica, Mediterranean forests are the world's smallest **biome.**

Mediterranean forests thrive where summers are hot and dry and winters mild and wet. Some trees shed their leaves as early as spring to survive the near-drought conditions of the summer. Most plants are low growing and have leathery leaves or thorns to **conserve** water. The tough leaves also keep grazing animals away.

Although fires are dangerous, they are important to the health of this **habitat.** Every 15 to 20 years the forests burn, which helps clear the dense thickets and allows new plants to grow, thus keeping life in this **ecosystem** in balance.

What's Cork?

You can probably think of several uses for cork, which comes from the bark of the cork oak tree. Cork floats and is both lightweight and waterproof. These qualities make it a useful material in life jackets, bottle stoppers, and even baseballs. Cork has been harvested around the Mediterranean for more than 2,000 years. It is peeled away from the tree with a special ax, then stacked in the sun to dry. Cork grows back stronger after each harvest and can be cut from the tree again every eight to 10 years.

Beautiful Blooms

Giant pink proteas grow in the fynbos of South Africa. Proteas come in many shapes, ranging from small trees to sprawling shrubs. They share the fynbos with 8,000 other types of flowering plants. Of those, 6,000 are found nowhere else on earth.

Ancient Lands

Forests near the Mediterranean Sea housed some of the world's first civilizations, including the Minoan, Greek, and Phoenician. Centuries of construction and agriculture have erased most of the original forest, but traces of the past remain, such as this ancient watchtower on the island of Mallorca.

What's in a Name?

Chaps

Chaps, the leather leggings worn by cowboys, get their name from a Basque word for Mediterranean-type scrubland, *chabbarra*. Chaps protect this cowboy's legs from the thorny thickets of the American Southwest.

Home on the Mallee

The mallee of southwestern Australia is dominated by low-growing eucalyptus trees that survive on an average of just 200 mm (8 in.) of rainfall per year. More than one-fifth of Australia was once covered with mallee, but much of that land is now covered by grasses from Europe and Asia and is used for grazing sheep.

Butcherbird

Woodchat shrikes impale small animals and insects on thorns before tearing them to bits. Such gruesome eating habits have caused these summertime residents of Mediterranean forests to be nicknamed butcherbirds.

Grasslands

When land is too wet to be a desert and too dry for trees to grow, grasses take over. Thriving on just 250 to 750 mm (10 to 30 in.) of rainfall each year, grasslands teem with life both aboveground and below, although the land may look deserted. Grasslands cover one-third of earth's land surface. On this **fertile** soil, the first humans learned to cultivate crops such as wheat and corn. Grain still makes up 70 percent of the world's food supply.

In fact, grasslands—called prairies, **savannas, pampas,** and steppes in different parts of the world—might more accurately be called farmlands now. Because of a growing human **population,** most stretches of wild grasses have been replaced by rows of crops. Wild grazing animals have largely been displaced by domesticated livestock. Even so, grasslands still shelter a multitude of wild animals.

Where in the World?

Steppe

Prairie

Savanna

Pampas

Grasslands

Last of the Tallgrass

Tallgrass prairies once covered more than 1 million sq km (400,000 sq mi.) of North America. Today only about 1 percent of that is left. The Tallgrass Prairie Preserve *(below)*, north of Tulsa, Oklahoma, looks much like the land in its original state because tough soil discouraged farming.

Friendly Fire

Would You *Believe?*

Without fire, grasslands would become choked with weeds, dead plants, and woodsy shrubbery. Lightning often causes grassland fires, but for millennia people at times have set them on purpose to clear the land for new growth.

Compare Grasses

Pampas Grass

The pampas grass of South America grows in large clumps, unlike most prairie grasses. Adorned with silvery plumes, it can grow to more than 3 m (10 ft.) tall.

Wheat

An early form of wheat was one of the grasses humans learned to cultivate, about 9,000 years ago. First grown in the Middle East, wheat is now a **staple** crop worldwide.

Big Bluestem

One of the tallest grasses of the American prairie is big bluestem. The grass grows as high as 2 m (7 ft.) and is a favorite of grazing cattle.

Enough for All?

Grass keeps growing from its roots even when cut. A shallow and spread-out root system lets the roots rapidly drink up any rain. During the dry season, grasses **conserve** water by staying dormant. Thus, grasslands offer a steady food supply to grazing animals, such as the cattle at left from Hungary's steppes.

But grasslands are in danger. The spread of human population has increased demand for live-stock as food and dairy sources. When too many animals graze in one area, the grass thins out and the soil is exposed to **erosion**.

The American Prairie

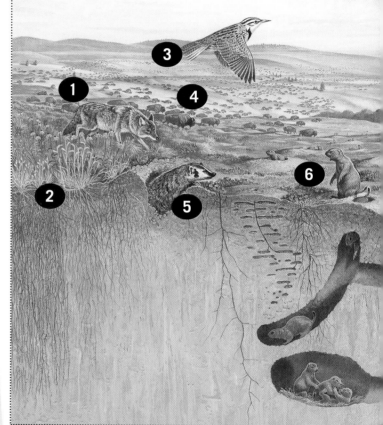

The North American prairie is a place of extremes. Scorching summers, freezing winters, and the lack of trees for lumber and firewood made life difficult for the first settlers there. But this vast grassland is a rich **ecosystem** with dozens of varieties of prairie grasses and hundreds of animal **species.** A prairie dog town *(right),* for example, supports a diverse **community.** As they dig their burrows, these rodents open up air passages in the soil, which makes grasses thrive for grazing animals, such as bison and antelope. The burrows also provide shelter for voles and ground squirrels. In turn, prairie dogs are prey for coyotes, badgers, weasels, and rattlesnakes. Ranchers, though, find prairie dogs a nuisance, because they compete with cattle for grass and breed rapidly. By mounting an attack on the prairie dog, they may wipe out a **predator** instead. But the absence of even a single species can throw the entire ecosystem out of balance. In 1901, a Texas town had 400 million prairie dogs living beneath it, because their predators had been eliminated.

Home of the Brave

This Shoshone Indian displays the horseback riding skills that helped make American Indians the first successful residents of the prairie. Taming these fast, durable mammals in the 17th and 18th centuries gave Indians, and later white settlers, easy means of transportation across the wide-open plains. Horses also helped in hunting, driving herds of cattle, and fighting wars.

Prairie Chicken

Drawn by a large **population** of insects, ground-nesting birds flock to the grasslands. The prairie chicken *(below)* ranges from the American plains north of Oklahoma to southern Canada. In its mating display, the male puffs out its chest and spreads its tail feathers.

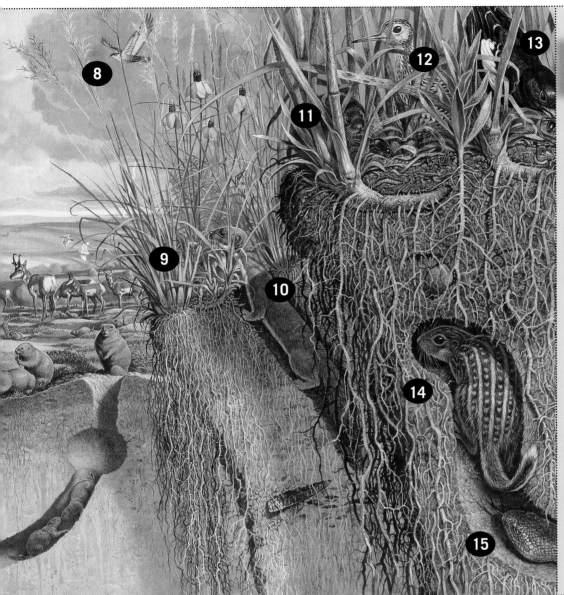

A prairie dog town amid dense grasses *(left)* attracts many species. Some of the animals listed below prey on the prairie dog for food. To cope with constant danger from above and below, prairie dogs have developed a complex language that includes a different warning call for each predator.

1. Coyote
2. Blue grama grass
3. Western meadowlark
4. Bison
5. Badger
6. Prairie dog
7. Pronghorn antelope
8. Hawk
9. Little bluestem grass
10. Weasel
11. Vole
12. Upland sandpiper
13. Lark bunting
14. Ground squirrel
15. Rattlesnake

Milking Milkweed

Early settlers of the prairie discovered that certain plants had medicinal benefits. Milkweed *(right)*, an herb that produces orange blossoms, was chewed by Omaha Indians and applied to wounds; white settlers used the roots to treat respiratory infections. Milkweed is also vital to the monarch butterfly, which depends on the plant for food and **habitat**.

Save the Ferret!

The black-footed ferret depends on the prairie dog for food and shelter. In the 1940s, when ranchers tried to get rid of prairie dogs, they nearly succeeded in killing off all the ferrets as well. A few ferrets were discovered in Wyoming recently and bred in captivity. More than 1,000 have now been returned to the wild, though they are still **endangered**.

Earth ALERT!

Savannas

Savannas are the world's tropical grasslands, covering large areas of Africa and Australia. These grasslands don't have the wide swings in temperature that prairies and steppes do, but they have alternating seasons of drought and rain.

Africa's savanna is famous for its wildlife. This is where you will find the largest, tallest, and fastest land animals—elephants, giraffes, cheetahs, rhinos, hippos, and lions. These exotic animals have been hunted nearly to extinction for their valuable furs, horns, and tusks.

Australia's **savanna** is much drier. What little grass there is supports the world's second-largest sheep **population** (China's is first). A few wild grazers such as the kangaroo and the emu, a flightless bird, also compete for food.

A herd of Burchell's zebras graze near an acacia tree in the Masai Mara National Reserve in Kenya. Africa's rainy season keeps the savanna wet enough to support a few drought-resistant trees.

People — Bernhard Grzimek

German zoologist Bernhard Grzimek, shown below with a bush baby, pioneered the global effort to **preserve** and protect wildlife. He came to fame by rebuilding the Frankfurt Zoo after World War II and filming documentaries on African wildlife, entitled *Serengeti Must Not Die.* But his greatest achievement surely is the creation of Serengeti National Park, a wildlife preserve where most of Africa's **endangered** large animals now live.

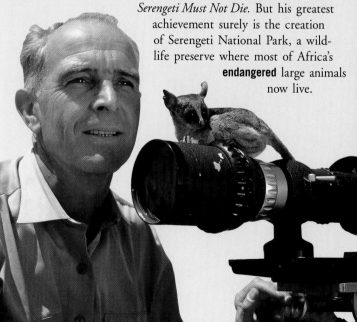

Hiding in the Open

Danger lies hidden in the Serengeti Plain for unsuspecting **prey.** Cheetahs can run up to 110 km/h (70 mph) to catch gazelles and antelope. They can race at top speed only for short stretches, so they must first get close to their prey. Their color and spots are an effective **camouflage** to hide them in the tall, yellowed savanna grass.

Ouch!

The spearlike thorns of the acacia tree help keep its branches from being stripped clean by large **browsers.** One animal that is not deterred, though, is the giraffe, whose thick, 0.6-m (2-ft.)-long tongue has no trouble with the thorns.

The Eagle Has Landed

It's not unusual to see birds foraging on the ground in the savanna. But skirmishes between a martial eagle and a warthog are rare. The warthog was trying to save its piglet from Africa's largest bird of prey. Although the warthog matched its tusks against the bird's talons, it lost the battle.

Masai Life

The Masai tribespeople of Kenya demonstrate one way to adapt to life in an area with few trees. They weave their homes from twigs, grass, and mud—the only plentiful material. Early settlers of the American prairie made do in similar ways by building houses of sod.

From Bountiful to Barren

A dramatic example of the fragile nature of grasslands is Africa's Sahel region, once a rich grazing land south of the Sahara. Drought and over-grazing by cattle and goats that eat the grasses down to their roots have turned the land to unproductive desert, causing widespread **famine.**

Pampas

The **pampas** of South America developed differently from grasslands in the rest of the world. Because South America was once a separate continent, not linked to other landmasses, the large hoofed animals that evolved in Africa and migrated to Europe, Asia, and North America never came here. Instead, the pampas' largest naturally occurring grazer is a bird—the rhea, a relative of the ostrich. And the main consumers of grasses on the pampas are hordes of insects, including termites, whose huge colonies aboveground and below help to churn and improve the soil.

When the landmasses of North and South America connected about three million years ago, the pampas slowly became more similar to the prairie. Really dramatic change came in the last two centuries. Where once there were wide-open spaces, there are now fenced-off farms and ranches with rows of cultivated crops and herds of domestic cattle.

Ride 'Em, Gauchos

Argentine gauchos drive a herd of beef cattle *(below)* —one of the country's most important exports. Once thought of as outlaws, gauchos became national heroes in Argentina's war against Spain in the early 1800s. Before the pampas were settled, gauchos learned to navigate the treeless plains by observing the direction of the equatorial winds, built fires using cow chips instead of wood, and became famous for their expert horsemanship.

Pampas Critters

GIANT ANTEATER

The giant anteater uses powerful claws to break into the mud castles of termites for food. At night it curls up in the grass, tucking its head between its legs and covering up with its fanlike tail.

MANED WOLF

Long legs help the maned wolf to see over tall grass in its search for food, which includes rodents, birds, and insects. This wolf, said to have a "lucky eye," has been hunted to near extinction for its magic.

ARMADILLO

Armadillos have adapted to life on the open plains by dining on insects and digging underground burrows. When threatened by **predators,** they roll into a ball, protected by their hard outer shell.

Alternating rows of soybeans and rice have replaced the wild grasses of this Brazilian grassland. Brazil is second only to the United States in exports of its agricultural products—one reason North and South America are called the breadbaskets of the world.

Let's Compare   Big Birds

Ostrich
The ostrich is the world's largest bird, standing nearly 3 m (10 ft.) tall. Like rheas and emus, ostriches have small wings but cannot fly. They use their long legs instead to run across the African **savanna.** They have been hunted for their exotic feathers.

Rhea
South America's rheas aren't as large as their ostrich cousins, but they do have similar social habits. During reproduction, the male builds a nest on the ground, into which several females lay eggs. The male then sits on the eggs until the new birds hatch.

Emu
The emu, an Australian flightless bird, uses its long legs to cover lots of feeding ground in the harsh **outback,** where its preferred diet of flowers, fruit, seeds, insects, and young grass can be scarce during the dry season.

Steppes

Stretching from Hungary in eastern Europe across China are grasslands called steppes, from the Russian word meaning "treeless plain." Steppes can be an unforgiving **environment,** buried by blizzards and dust storms in winter and as hot and dry as a desert in summer. Only sturdy animals like the Bactrian camel are suited to this harsh climate. The people who have inhabited the steppes had a long tradition of nomadic life. They were always on the move because of the constant need to escape the elements and find food for their livestock.

Before the last ice age, around 11,000 years ago, the steppes looked much like today's African **savanna.** Huge grazers like the woolly mammoth lived here, preyed on by cave lions and saber-toothed cats. But this part of the world became too cold and dry to support such large herbivores and their **predators.** Eventually, as with every other grassland, much of the steppes was converted to farmland.

What's Falconry?

Falconry is the ancient sport of using birds of prey for hunting. Before the age of firearms, falconry was an efficient way to hunt game birds and rabbits across the wide-open steppes, and trained birds were prized by kings. A few Asians still practice this dangerous craft; some even train birds as large as golden eagles *(above).*

Exposed to the Elements

Blizzards can quickly turn green pastures into barren white expanses, making life difficult for Mongolian nomads and their cattle. Almost half of Mongolia's two million people live as nomads, coping with one of the most unpredictable environments on earth.

Mongols at War

In the 13th century, China, Russia, and parts of Europe were invaded and conquered by hordes of warriors from the remote region of Mongolia. Genghis Khan had united his nomadic countrymen into an army whose skill on horse-back, hunting prowess, and durability—all trademarks of survival on the steppes—made them a terrifying new force. The Mongol Empire was the largest in history until the British Empire of the 19th century.

Pastoral Life

Karakul sheep, like this flock grazing in Qonduz, Afghanistan, are prized for their wool during the central Asian winters. On the steppes, domesticated animals have all but replaced wild animals, who compete for limited food and water.

Wild Horses

The steppes were home to earth's last undomesticated horse, Przewalski's horse, which disappeared from the wild in 1947. About 1,000 were bred in captivity, and recently the **species** was reintroduced into its former **habitat.**

Fabulous **Features!**

Europe's only antelope, the saiga, has adapted to life on the steppes in some unusual ways. Its bulbous nose contains a large, mucus-lined sac in each nostril to warm and moisten cold, dry air. Females, such as the one below with her calf, are able to give birth when only seven months old, and often have twins. During winter, most males starve themselves, leaving the limited food supply to females to ensure the survival of the species.

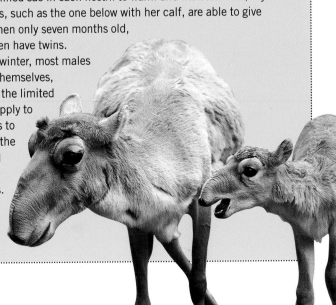

Wetlands

Just as water is vital to life, wetlands—areas covered by water for most of the year—are vital to the world. Wetlands provide **habitat** and breeding grounds for thousands of plants and animals, making them key features of every landscape—even deserts! Though we tend to think of wetlands as brackish swamps near the sea, they may be found thousands of miles inland and range from puny marshes to mighty rivers. Some wetlands contain salt water and some contain fresh water.

Without wetlands, humans could not exist. Two-thirds of the fish we eat live and feed in wetlands. So does another food **staple**—rice—which grows only in warm, moist conditions.

Wetlands also soak up runoff from storms, keeping floods in check, and act as natural water purifiers, absorbing harmful chemicals and filtering out wastes.

Where in the World?

Wetlands

Let's Compare

Swamp A wetland covered with standing water most of the time and dominated by trees is known as a swamp. Most swamps form in low-lying areas with high water levels.

Marsh A wetland dominated by tall-grasses rather than trees is called a marsh. Like a swamp, a marsh may contain either salt water or fresh water.

Bog A wetland with poor drainage that is waterlogged year round is termed a bog. Instead of grass or trees, bogs are packed with moss.

Ice Marked the Spot

A prairie pothole *(below)* is a watery depression that was gouged out by **glaciers** during the last ice age some 12,000 years ago. These unusual wetlands dot the Great Plains of the United States and Canada, where farmers plant their crops around them. Prairie potholes are prime breeding sites for waterfowl in flyways between the northern and southern plains.

Try it!

Homegrown Wetlands

All you need to create your own **ecosystem** is a shovel and a sunny spot! Unlike a **forest** or a grassland, a wetland can be as small as a backyard pool. Just 45 cm (18 in.) of water will support water lilies, birds, dragonflies, and frogs. A row of rocks around the edge will give the pond a finished look.

Flamingos

A flock of flamingos cluster on the **soda**-encrusted shores of Tanzania's Natron Lake. Typical of wetlands worldwide, the lake is home to millions of birds. Unlike other wetlands, however, it contains lethal levels of soda that keep other creatures away. Porous bills let the flamingos safely strain nutritious minerals and **algae** from the **alkaline** water.

Marshes

arshes are dominated by tallgrasses such as cattails and bulrushes. They may look like placid places, but in truth they are hives of violence and death. Dragonflies and mosquitoes are snatched from midair by feeding frogs, who in turn may be gobbled up by snakes. Stalking these lower creatures nonstop are water birds such as herons and egrets: The sharp-eyed hunters use their long legs as stilts to wade through standing water, and their pointed bills as harpoons to spear unwary victims.

Marshes come in both fresh- and saltwater versions. All land plants need fresh water to live, however, so salt marsh grasses catch and store rainwater whenever it falls. If that rainfall is scarce, a shallow marsh may dry up. When that happens, alligators may come to the rescue. They use their powerful tails to thrash out holes, which then can collect water again and form miniature wetlands of their own.

The Everglades

On the lookout for passing prey, a great blue heron gazes out over a saw grass marsh in Everglades National Park in southern Florida. The Everglades cover 34,000 sq km (13,000 sq mi.) of varied wetlands. Only 5,000 sq km (2,000 sq mi.) are protected from development.

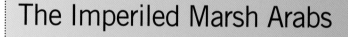

Marsh Marauder

A Bengal tiger prowls an Indian marsh in search of **prey.** Though typically thought of as jungle creatures, Bengal tigers prefer wet grasslands such as this one. They are excellent swimmers—and happy to get their feet wet when the payoff is a fresh kill.

The Imperiled Marsh Arabs

Ma'dan visitors arrive at a village in the isolated marshes of southern Iraq. The houses are built from reeds, which are woven into mats, fences, and walls. The Ma'dan, or Marsh Arabs, have lived in these wetlands for more than 5,000 years, but their way of life is in peril. Iraq has built dams and canals to divert water from the Tigris and Euphrates Rivers for crops, threatening to drain the Ma'dan from their ancient homeland.

People

Friend of the Everglades

A fierce defender of the Florida Everglades, writer Marjory Stoneman Douglas spent most of her 108 years fighting for their protection. She began in the 1920s and sat next to President Harry S Truman as he dedicated Everglades National Park in 1947. Dissatisfied with the pace of preservation, however, she founded the group Friends of the Everglades in 1969 and promoted the cause until her death in 1998. Where most people saw a stagnant marsh, she found a lush paradise teeming with wildlife such as the graceful anhinga below. Called snake-bird because only its head and neck show when it swims, the anhinga lacks the oil glands that most birds use to repel water. After a swim, it perches with its wings spread wide to dry off.

Let's Compare

Coastal Marsh

Two bittern hatchlings *(right)* huddle with a last egg in the nest in a salt marsh. Incoming tides from the ocean bring a steady flow of salt water, enriched with fish and shellfish, into these marshes, providing the right diet for these ground-nesting birds.

Freshwater Marsh

Freshwater marshes lie inland, usually near lakes and rivers. They abound with specialized plants such as the water lilies at right. The lilies' broad leaves float on the surface to capture air, which travels through a soft stem to reach the plants' roots underwater.

Swamps

A swamp is a low-lying area blanketed with water and trees. Most swamps form in warm regions near a lake or stream where the water runoff is slow. In the United States, swamps are common in the Southeast. In South America, extensive swamplands surround the Amazon River basin. African swamps abound beside the Congo River.

Although the trees in a swamp vary with its location, they all must be able to grow in standing water. A bald cypress tree, for instance, has knobs that extend from the base and stick up out of the water; these "knees," as they are known, may absorb **oxygen** and transfer it to the rest of the tree's roots.

Swamps swarm with amphibious animals—those that spend as much time in the water as out. Toads and frogs, turtles and snakes, beavers and muskrats, wading birds, and insects are all typical.

Plant Life

Paperbark Tree

Swamps in Southeast Asia often are overgrown with clumps of paperbark trees (*left*). They are named for the thin strips of bark near their base that give additional support in their watery **habitat.**

Spanish Moss

Strands of Spanish moss festoon a live oak tree in a swamp in Georgia. Lacking roots, Spanish moss draws water and **nutrients** from rain, dust, and the surrounding air.

Animal Life

A Paddler

A proboscis monkey paddles its way across a swamp in Borneo, Indonesia. Though known for their long, flexible snout, proboscis monkeys also have webbed hind feet that suit them to wetland life.

Swamp Thing

Botswana's Okavango Swamp shelters more than 500 bird **species,** among them the saddle-billed stork (*right*). Standing 1.5 m (5 ft.) tall, it snares fish, frogs, and small reptiles with its long bill.

A Floating Carpet

Pond scum? No—that green carpet on the wetland canal below is duckweed—a small floating plant that ducks love to eat. Because duckweed filters man-made **pollutants** from the water, it is a priceless natural purifier.

Night Lights

Alligator eyes—set aglow by a camera flash—pierce the darkness of a Florida swamp. More than 200 gators were forced to gather in this deep pool by a drought that dried up their wetlands from December 1988 to May 1990. Alligators and their crocodile cousins can exert 14.4 t (16 tn.) of force with their jaws. As shown by the crocodile at lower right, however, both reptiles are gentle enough to carry their eggs, and even their young, in their mouths.

Bogs and Fens

Unlike swamps, which occur in warm, southern climates, bogs and fens occupy cooler, northern regions. One key factor separates the two: Fens receive **nutrients** from **ground water,** but bogs do not. Although bogs are so acidic that they support little life, dead plants that decompose slowly in them often settle on the bottom, where they turn into peat—an organic soil that can be burned for fuel. Bogs produce peat in such abundance that they are sometimes called peat-lands. In Ireland, for example, peat is cut and burned to furnish 40 percent of the country's electricity.

Bogs are not infinite resources, so they must be protected. They store carbon, reducing the level of **carbon dioxide** in the atmosphere. Bogs also emit large amounts of **oxygen.** That is why bogs have been dubbed the lungs of the earth.

What's in a Name?

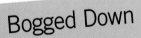

Bogged Down

The fate of this rowboat—marooned and abandoned in a bog—shows why "bogged down" has come to mean "mired in an unpleasant situation." The soft, squishy mat of waterlogged vegetation in a bog acts almost like quick-sand. Animals and people have perished—and been preserved—in bogs. Scientists in Denmark found the body of a man who had fallen into a peat bog 2,000 years ago. The bog's oxygen-poor soil preserved the man's body so well that his stomach still held the last meal he ate.

Tourist Trap?

The windmills of northern Europe—including this one on the River Ant in Norfolk, England—attract tourists to the windblown fens and bogs year round. Unfortunately, the delicate wetland **ecosystems** cannot withstand the heavy foot traffic that results. Overfishing also damages these types of **environments**.

What Lives in a Bog?

A STARRY NOSE

Despite its alien appearance, the star-nosed mole *(above)* is a harmless bog dweller. The 22 tentacles surrounding its snout help the poor-sighted mammal find worms and insects underground.

NATURE'S SPONGE

Most plants would die in the acid bogs, but sphagnum moss thrives, adding to the acidity by excreting antibiotics. Bogs are so waterlogged because sphagnum moss can hold 10 times its weight in water.

DEWDROP INN

Plants such as the sundew have adapted to the lack of nutrients in bogs by becoming carnivores. They ooze sticky droplets that lure insects into tentacles, where the bugs are digested.

Where on EARTH?

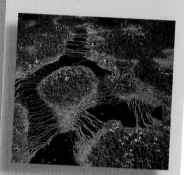

A Tangled Web

Ribbons of sedge grass radiate like bicycle spokes from the center of a fen in Labrador, Canada. Scientists have not yet figured out how water flow and plant growth combine to create this and other odd formations in fens and bogs around the world.

Cranberry Bogs

A wetland need not be wild to have value. This commercial cranberry bog in South Carver, Massachusetts, has become a favorite nesting spot for kestrels, bluebirds, and ospreys.

Estuaries

Estuaries exist in places where a river's current meets an ocean's tide. The living conditions here are harsh. Tides rush in and out, and the water is salty. But estuaries are diverse **habitats.** When the tide is in, sea creatures are in, too. When the tide is out, land animals roam.

In **temperate** regions, estuaries are marked by mud flats—the land exposed during low tide. The largest mud flats in the world—those along the North Sea *(right)*—stretch 10 km (6 mi.) from shore. (Pack a dinghy if you walk out that far!) In tropical regions, by contrast, an estuary's defining features are mangrove swamps—large stands of trees whose roots grow above the water *(opposite page, lower right)*. Both **habitats** are ecological linchpins: Mud flats harbor underground animals that decompose organic waste, whereas mangroves protect coastlines from hurricanes.

Earth ALERT!

Flying Lessons

Even birds need directions sometimes! To reestablish trumpeter swans in the eastern United States, scientists trained some of the young wetland birds to follow an ultralight plane as if it were their mother *(below)*. The ultralight then flew from New York State to Maryland's Chesapeake Bay, teaching the swans their historic migration pattern.

From Mud to Mainland

As a river flows into an estuary, the water slows down and deposits sediments it has been carrying. Larger rock or sand grains, being heavier, are dropped first in areas farthest from the ocean. As they pile up, a new section of land forms, and salt grasses *(above)* take root in it. This process is called succession.

The Right Bill for the Job

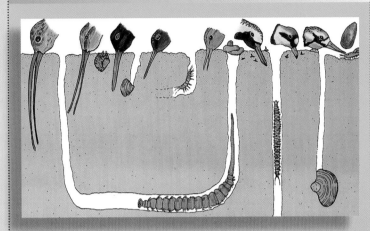

Mud flats seem barren, but they teem with life below the surface —to the delight of hungry shorebirds. Because their bills differ in length, the birds do not compete for the same food. The short bill of a plover, for example, is ideal for nabbing snails near the surface; the curlew, by contrast, uses its long bill to dig deep for lugworms.

Life at Ebb Tide

The mangrove swamps of Indonesia and West Africa are home to the mudskipper *(above)*—an odd fish that can survive out of water, scamper across mud flats, and shin its way up tree trunks.

The oystercatcher *(left)* pokes its sharp bill into oysters during the brief moment at ebb tide when their shells are open.

An Asmat fisherman *(below)* displays his recent catch—a large swamp crab—in a mangrove forest in Irian Jaya, Indonesia. The Asmat people use canoes carved from tree trunks to travel through these densely wooded wetlands, where fishing is their livelihood.

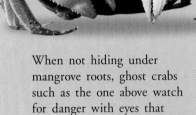

When not hiding under mangrove roots, ghost crabs such as the one above watch for danger with eyes that give them 360-degree vision.

Rivers Lakes and Ponds

Rivers are cradles of civilization. The ancient societies of Mesopotamia, China, and Egypt all grew up in the **fertile** land around rivers, which provided food, water, and transportation. Rivers are also a key link in earth's water cycle: They send fresh water to the sea, where it evaporates and returns to the land as rain. As humans have tried to "civilize" rivers—that is, to dam them for power or wall them in for flood control—they have discovered that they cause problems in a complex **environment.**

Lakes are the largest standing-water wetlands of all. Unlike rivers, they may contain either fresh water or salt water. Many lakes are geographic scars of past cataclysms: They were gouged out by **glaciers** or exploding volcanoes. Ponds are small-scale lakes. Their lesser volume makes their water level apt to change, a shift that harms most freshwater wetlands.

What's an Oxbow?

Sometimes a river flows so sluggishly that it forms loops. An oxbow forms when the river carves a new straight channel at one of its bends *(above)* and flows past the loop. During heavy rains, the river will overflow into the interior of the loop, forming a shallow lake. During a drought it may dry up and fill in with plants.

A Cleaned-Up Rhine

From its humble origin as a trickle of water high in the Swiss Alps, the Rhine River becomes one of Europe's mightiest waterways: It winds 1,320 km (820 mi.) through Austria, France, Germany, and the Netherlands before emptying into the North Sea. Dumping by five nations had polluted the river so much that by 1976 there was no life left. But Europeans launched a successful cleanup and the river is alive again with fish.

Flying Fisher

Would You Believe?

This Japanese fisherman leaves his rod and reel at home when he goes fishing on the Nagara River. Instead, he loads his boat with trained fishing birds known as cormorants. The fisherman ties one end of a string to his boat, then loops the other end around a cormorant's neck. Drawing the string just tight enough to let the bird breathe and swallow small fish, the fisherman releases the bird into the water to catch the large fish for him.

Water Damage

The Hoover Dam, on the border of Arizona and Nevada, harnesses the Colorado River, providing water and electricity to millions of people in the West. But the once mighty river now ends in a trickle *(left)* about 30 km (20 mi.) short of its original mouth on the Gulf of California, Mexico.

How **Big?**

Giant Lily Pads

Almost 2 m (7 ft.) across, the pads of the Amazon water lily *(above)* are strong enough to hold a child without sinking. Each pad owes its strength to a web of veins, full of air pockets, that grow on the underside. This remarkably lightweight yet sturdy design inspired much of the steel-beam architecture that holds up modern cities.

Emperor of the Pond

An emperor dragonfly—one sign of a healthy freshwater wetland—clings to a stalk of cordgrass. Largest of all the dragonflies, the emperor as an adult can overtake and capture other insects in midair; even most birds cannot catch it. The adult stage lasts only four weeks—long enough for mating. Before that, the emperor spends most of its life—about two years—as a larva underwater.

A Mexican Oasis

A desert—known for its lack, not abundance, of water—seems the least likely place for a wetland. But in northern Mexico lies a rare wetland, known as Cuatro Ciénegas (Four Marshes), that has been called Mexico's desert aquarium. Recognizing what a rare **environment** this is, the Mexican government set aside Cuatro Ciénegas *(pictured on this page)* as a biological reserve in 1994.

Hot springs are another offbeat wetland. Their near-boiling temperatures are hostile to larger life forms, but microscopic **bacteria** known as **thermophiles** (heat lovers) thrive in the hot water. These bacteria can also tolerate a hot spring's high acidity and high mineral levels. Indeed, some thermophiles have been known to double their **population** in as little as two hours!

One of a Kind

A Coahuilan box turtle *(below)* sniffs the desert air from its underwater home in the "**arid** wetland" of Cuatro Ciénegas, Mexico. Unlike all other box turtles, which evolved into land reptiles, the Coahuilan box turtle spends a lot of time submerged. **Aquatic** plants and small fish provide it plenty of food.

Getting in Hot Water

Surrounded by the searing Chihuahuan Desert, a snorkeler enjoys a spring-fed pool at Cuatro Ciénegas. Because this freshwater oasis is fed by water rising from deep underground, it contains no sediment and is so clear it offers almost unlimited visibility.

Hot Springs

Wyoming's Yellowstone National Park boasts the world's highest concentration of hot springs. One of the most impressive is Grand Prismatic Spring *(below)*, whose center reaches a steamy 93°C (199°F). That's too hot for insects, crustaceans, and multicellular plants—they die at 49°C (120°F)—but some organisms called thermophiles *(left)* thrive in the center of the hot pool. On the slightly cooler fringes, multicolored bacteria form a flaming pattern.

Faces of the Desert

When you think of a desert, you probably imagine a hot, dry place with cacti or sand dunes. But that is only one kind of desert. You can see on the map below that there are four major types of deserts. And they all look different: Some are mostly stone or gravel, others have many kinds of plants, and some are not hot at all. In a way, even the entire continent of Antarctica—the coldest place on earth—is a desert! One thing all of the world's deserts have in common is a lack of rain—250 mm (10 in.) per year or less. With so little water, vegetation is scarce. The land is exposed directly to the sun and wind. Without trees or grasses to break the wind, desert landscapes suffer far more **erosion** than other regions, and temperatures **fluctuate** greatly between daytime and night.

Where in the World?

Deserts

- Cold Winter Deserts
- Polar Deserts
- Subtropical Deserts
- Cool Coastal Deserts

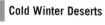

Fast FACTS

Driest Desert Atacama Desert (Chile): average annual rainfall less than 0.08 mm (0.003 in.)

Largest Desert Sahara (North Africa): 9,064,959 sq km (3,500,000 sq mi.)

Coldest Desert Antarctica: average temperature -58.2°C (-72°F)

Hottest Recorded Temperature Al-'Aziziya, Libya (Sahara): 58°C (136°F)

Highest Desert Gobi (Mongolia): up to 1,500 m (5,000 ft.)

Lowest Desert Desert surrounding the Dead Sea in Israel: 400 m (1,300 ft.) below sea level

Largest Cactus Saguaro cactus (Arizona): up to 17 m (57 ft.) tall

Largest Sand Dune Isaouane 'n Tifernine, Algeria (Sahara): 5 km (3 mi.) long and up to 465 m (1,525 ft.) high

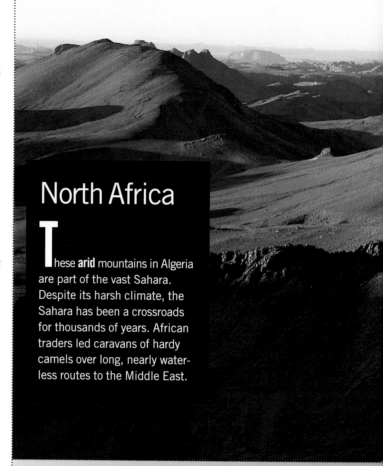

North Africa

These **arid** mountains in Algeria are part of the vast Sahara. Despite its harsh climate, the Sahara has been a crossroads for thousands of years. African traders led caravans of hardy camels over long, nearly waterless routes to the Middle East.

Arabian Peninsula

You can see from the map that the deserts of the Arabian Peninsula are really an extension of the Sahara. The area shown below in Saudi Arabia is known by the Arabic name of Rub 'al-Khali, which means "the Empty Quarter." About the size of Texas, this desert contains the largest body of sand in the world.

Strange But TRUE!

Flash Floods

At times, when rain comes to the desert, the barren, often salt-encrusted land cannot soak it up fast enough, resulting in dangerous flash floods. In North America, more people drown in the deserts every year than die of thirst!

Making Tracks

The sidewinder rattlesnake of the North American desert can move quickly over slippery dunes. The snake coils its body into several loops that touch the hot sand only in two or three places at a time.

North America

A farmer walks his horse among rolling tumbleweeds in the Sonoran Desert, the largest and hottest in North America. Sonora, a Native American word that means "place of plants," includes parts of the south-western United States and Mexico. To grow crops or raise livestock in this climate, farmers must **irrigate** the land with water either from deep wells or from one of the region's rivers.

North American Deserts

JAVELINA

North America contains two distinct types of desert. The Great Basin of Nevada is a cold winter desert. The land is high in elevation and lies in the shadow of the towering Sierra Nevada, making for a cold but very dry climate.

The Sonoran and Mojave Deserts of the southwestern United States and the Chihuahuan Desert of Mexico are another, more common type of desert, called **subtropical.** They are home to a surprising variety of plant and animal life that has adapted to scorching heat, broiling sun, and little rain. Many animals spend the day underground, coming out to feed at dawn and dusk when the temperature is lower. Plants have adapted by developing deep roots to tap buried water or broad, shallow root systems that quickly drink up rain when it falls. Some plants called succulents store water in their stems or leaves; others changed their leaves to spines to **conserve** water.

Earth ALERT !

Threats to a Fragile Land

Racing through the desert in dune buggies and other all-terrain vehicles (ATVs) has become a popular sport. Unfortunately, the vehicles can have a serious impact on the delicate desert **ecosystem.** Exhaust from the engines pollutes the clean desert air. Tires can destroy plant life or break down the delicate structure of desert soils. The vehicles' weight also compacts the soil, sometimes making it impossible for new seedlings to gain a foothold.

Life in the Desert

The stately saguaro cactus and the yellow-flowered brittlebush *(below)* thrive in Arizona's Sonoran Desert after a spring rain. Saguaros are **endangered** because some homeowners obtain them illegally for use as decorative plants in their yards. The yucca cactus *(above)* at White Sands, New Mexico, digs its roots deep into the desert soil in search of water.

Hardy Creatures

SPIDER

The wolf spider, named for its wolflike habit of pouncing on its **prey,** builds its nest underground to escape the desert heat. The spider's eight eyes make it easier to hunt for food in the dark.

A white-tailed antelope squirrel wound up with a faceful of needles after feeding on a cholla cactus in California's Mojave Desert.

SQUIRREL

The javelina *(opposite),* a wild pig, hides among rocks or in caves during midday and comes out in the evening to dig plant roots and bulbs out of the soil with its snout.

OWL

An elf owl makes a cozy nest high in a saguaro cactus. These desert owls often move into abandoned holes drilled by Gila woodpeckers.

The Gila monster *(below)* is the largest—and only poisonous —lizard found in the United States. It eats rodents, small birds, and reptile eggs and uses the poison glands in its lower jaw mainly in defense or for hunting.

LIZARD

Subtropical Deserts

North Africa's Sahara

The hottest places on earth are the **subtropical** deserts. Although you would expect them to spread out along the hot **equator,** they lie farther north and south of the equator. These deserts are created by wind patterns. As the earth spins on its axis, it creates giant swirling air currents in the atmosphere (*pages 24-25*). Hot air rises from the equator and flows northward and southward, cooling as it moves toward the polar regions. When this cooler air descends, it warms and picks up moisture, drying out the land.

As you can see from the map on page 68, this movement of warm air masses has created two belts of subtropical deserts around the globe. In the Northern Hemisphere they include the Sahara in Africa, the Rub 'al-Khali in Saudi Arabia, the Thar Desert in India, and the Mojave, Sonoran, and Chihuahuan Deserts in North America. In the Southern Hemisphere they are the Kalahari Desert in southern Africa and the **outback** of Australia. These fragile lands, once seen as wastelands, compose a valuable and complex **ecosystem** and are home to many nomadic people.

San Hunter

The San hunters of southern Africa's Kalahari Desert are skilled at finding food and water in their parched homeland. This hunter had stored an empty ostrich egg in a pit underground. Weeks later he can use a straw to drink the water that collected. The nomadic San will set up a circular camp of huts on a spot that offers a supply of wild plants or nearby herds of game. There is no surface water in the Kalahari except during the brief rainy season. The San's other source of liquids is from roots, tubers, and the leaves of succulent plants.

Camel Fair in India

A woman bargains for camel fodder at the Pushkar open-air market. Camel caravans travel regularly past this town at the edge of the Thar Desert in northwestern India. Camels are the only pack animals that can stand the daytime temperatures of 49°C (120°F) or more. Still, most caravans travel at night when the temperature drops to about 25°C (77°F).

At certain places in the Sahara where underground springs bring water to the surface, lush groves of date palms thrive. This island of green *(below)* in the middle of a sea of sand is called an oasis.

Australia's water-holding frog has a unique way of surviving the dry season in the desert. It can store up to 50 percent of its body weight in water under a layer of dead skin. The native people, called Aborigines, use the frogs' water as emergency "canteens" during a drought.

Chameleon

Tiptoeing over the hot desert sand, an African flap-necked chameleon prowls for insects; it catches its **prey** with its long tongue. Like other reptiles the chameleon is a **cold-blooded** animal that relies on its surroundings for warmth. Reptiles are specially suited to life in the desert, because their scaly skin keeps in body moisture.

Australia

Five separate subtropical deserts cover most of the continent of Australia. Taken together these **arid** lands are called the outback. In many areas, the reddish soil is dotted with clumps of *Spinifex,* a razor-sharp grass *(left).* The outback is home to Australia's largest remaining **predator,** the dingo, a breed of wild dog found only on the island continent.

Coastal Deserts

Atacama in South America

Some desert areas are caused by ocean currents rather than wind patterns. The earth's rotation causes ocean waters to flow in a vast circular motion called oceanic gyres. As cold water from Antarctica moves northward through the Atlantic and Pacific Oceans toward the **equator,** it comes into contact with the western edges of Africa and South America.

The air over the cold ocean water cools as it moves toward land. The strong sea winds that blow ashore frequently bring fog, but they seldom bring rain. These conditions have created two of the driest, most forbidding places on earth—the Namib Desert of southwestern Africa and the Atacama Desert in Chile. The few plants and animals that can survive there rely mostly on what little moisture they can get from fog.

Because the coastlines of these deserts are often shrouded in mist, they have been a graveyard for many wrecked ships and their crews over the centuries. That is why the Namib has been nicknamed the Skeleton Coast.

A rare rainfall in northern Chile brings forth a small patch of life in the desert *(left)*. The flowers have pushed up through the cracked bed of a lake that contains water only part of the year. When the lake evaporates, the mud dries out and contracts, breaking into uneven shapes. The barren strip of South American coast called the Atacama *(below)* is the driest spot on earth.

Flamingos

A flock of wild flamingos soar over a 3,650-m (12,000-ft.)-high pass on the western slope of the rugged Andes Mountains in the Atacama Desert. They are only visitors there. Flamingos build conical nests of mud in salt lakes found high in the Andes and feed along the desert's coast on microscopic **algae** and small **invertebrates** that they strain through their bills.

Africa's Namib

You might be surprised to learn that elephants live in the Namib. Over time, their bodies have adapted to the dry desert **environment.** They are the tallest elephants in the world and can go for several days without water while traveling long distances between **springs.**

Living Rocks

Plants in the Namib found amazing ways to adapt to the desert. Most of the stone plant grows underground, where it is protected from the desert heat. To fool grazing animals, it produces two round, fleshy leaves that look like rocks.

Desert Animals and Plants

Bat-Eared Fox

This desert fox is one of the few mammals able to tolerate the harsh conditions of the Namib. The large, batlike ears help radiate heat away from its body.

Welwitschia

This strange plant with large, leathery leaves is found only in the Namib. The plant's sole source of moisture is the coastal fog. The largest specimens measure 8 m (26 ft.) across and are 2,000 years old.

Cold Winter and Polar Deserts

Mountain ranges can also cause deserts to form by producing a special climatic condition called a rain shadow. As the wind pushes clouds upward over one side of the mountains, they cool and lose their moisture in the form of rain and snow. The air that flows down the other side not only carries no rain, it is so dry that it evaporates moisture from the soil. The Great Basin and Colorado Plateau of the American West and the Patagonian Desert in Argentina are examples of this process.

Other deserts, like those in central Asia and China, formed because the winds over those regions are far from large bodies of water and have lost much of their moisture. Because all these deserts are far from the hot tropics, they have cold winter climates. Some scientists say that the coldest deserts of all are in the Arctic and Antarctica. Although most of the land is covered with frozen water there, it still receives less than 13 mm (0.5 in.) of **precipitation** a year.

Polar Valley

A very small percentage of Antarctica's landmass consists of valleys where constant winds have scoured away the ice and snow, exposing the soil etched into patterns by the permanent frost. The British explorer Robert Scott was the first to discover these dry valleys in 1903. "Below lay the sandy stretches and confused boulder heaps of the valley floor," he wrote in his journal. "It is worthy of record, too, that we have seen no living thing, not even a moss or a lichen."

Central Asia

The deserts in the high mountains of Afghanistan *(above)* and Iran *(below)* are so cold and bleak that one area between the two countries is called the Desert of Death. Camels and horses are the best means of transportation there.

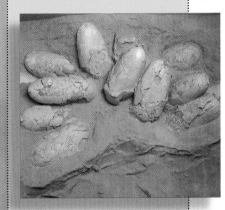

Dinosaur Eggs

The lack of plant cover makes desert regions a good place to look for fossils. The *Protoceratops* eggs shown above were found in the Gobi Desert. When these dinosaurs were alive some 90 million years ago, the Gobi was a greener place, probably covered by salt marshes.

Cold Desert Dwellers

Unlike the animals that live in **subtropical** deserts, most residents of cold winter deserts are active during daylight hours and seek shelter at night. Both the caracal, or desert lynx *(right)*, and the monitor lizard *(below)* have adapted to the **arid** regions of central Asia.

I Was There!

"A desert traveler in the Gobi Desert of China may hear drums and the clash of arms—spirits talking in such a way that they seem to be his companions. They seem to force soldiers and explorers to close their line of march and to proceed in a more compact order for protection."

—*Marco Polo, Venetian explorer who crossed central Asia by horse, donkey, and camel in the 13th century*

Mountains

Not only do mountains tower above the land surrounding them, they affect it in many ways. They influence temperature and rainfall, harbor threatened **species** of plants and animals, and offer inspiration and material resources to many unique human cultures.

Mountains can be created by a number of geological forces, and each type of mountain affects its **environment** differently. Volcanoes, for example, cause destruction, but their ashes produce **fertile** soils, inviting lush plant life. Another type, called fault and fold mountains, bring seams of precious metal and minerals close to the surface for mining. Most important, mountains control climate and the water supply around them. The cold peaks create their own weather patterns, block rain clouds, or create fog from water in the atmosphere. Forested slopes retain heavy rainfalls, protecting lowlands from floods. A warm season may melt **glaciers** and snowfields, causing floods, avalanches, or landslides.

Where in the World?

Mountains

Fast FACTS

Highest Mountain Mount Everest in the Himalaya of Asia stands 8,848 m (29,028 ft.) tall.

Longest Range The Andes of South America stretch 8,000 km (5,000 mi.).

Oldest Mountains The Appalachians of North America began to rise more than 430 million years ago.

Fastest Growing Parícutin volcano in Mexico grew 150 m (490 ft.) in seven days, 410 m (1,350 ft.) in nine years.

Most Dangerous A landslide in the mountains of Gansu Province, China, killed 180,000 people in 1920.

STORING WATER

Glaciers, such as the one below in British Columbia, Canada, and snowcaps on mountaintops can keep water bound up as ice for many millennia. Mountain lakes, sometimes dammed up to generate electric power, also regulate water flow to the lowlands.

AVALANCHES

Avalanches—like this one in 1997 in Galtür, Austria, about to bury a house—occur when steep slopes hold a heavy layer of snow on top of weaker ones. Noise, an earth tremor, or new snowfall triggers the slides that destroy everything in their path.

RAIN SHADOWS

Clouds moving eastward on prevailing winds over high mountains behind the Annapurna Range in the Himalaya meet high cold air and condense into rain on the western slopes. Rain seldom reaches the **arid** desert on the eastern—the rain shadow—side.

Would **You** *Believe?*

Katabatic Winds

Scientists call them katabatic winds, but the winds go by many names: Santa Ana in Los Angeles, *mistral* in France, and *Föhn* in the Alps. They drop down mountain slopes at up to 320 km/h (200 mph), tearing off roofs, uprooting trees, and fanning disastrous brush fires in southern California *(left)*. Some people claim the winds cause headaches and depression, calling them the "winds that drive you crazy."

Mountain Types

Uplift

The jagged peaks of the Teton Range in Wyoming were thrust upward when one continental plate rose up over the edge of an adjoining plate. The slanted seams of rock that once lay level are clearly visible.

Fault and Fold

Many mountain ranges were created by continental plates pressing against one another. The force bends the earth's surface into folds like these on South Georgia Island, near Antarctica. Folds may break, stand on end, or form piles.

Dome

Molten rock, called magma, from the earth's interior can bulge up under surface rock, raising it above the surrounding area. The result is dome mountains, like South Dakota's Black Hills *(left)*.

Volcano

Volcanoes form where magma flows up through weak spots in the earth's crust, making a cone shape, as at Ecuador's Mount Cotopaxi *(right)*. Many famous peaks, among them Mount Fuji in Japan and Vesuvius in Italy, are volcanic in origin.

Mountains Close up

Coping on the Heights

Though they may look empty, most mountains support dense **communities** of plants and animals, and in some places people. Covering a fifth of earth's land surface, mountains are home to one-tenth of its human **population.** In the past, animals and plants threatened by changing climates have found new refuges in the mountains. The range of **habitats** from low to high altitudes results in great **biodiversity** in a small area—and plenty of mixing among groups of the same **species.** Mountains also shelter wild populations of plants and animals that have been driven out of the lowlands by disease or farming practices. The highland survivors serve as **gene pools** for improving lowland plants and breeding disease-resistant animals. But mountain **environments** are fragile, because they contain young, easily **eroded** soils, extremes of heat and cold, and **oxygen**-poor air. Logging, mining, tourism, and new farms on high slopes damage both the mountain community and those nearby in the lowlands.

Animals and plants living on high mountains have to cope with extreme temperature changes; thin, rocky soil; high levels of **ultraviolet radiation;** and scanty food supplies. Here are some brilliant survival strategies, evolved over many thousands of years.

Plants

Alpine Snowbells

Flowers such as alpine snowbells form blossom buds at the end of each short summer season, so they are ready to bloom in spring. As soon as the snow thins a little, they pop up and offer early meals to hungry pollinating insects.

Saussurea

The *Saussurea* growing in the Himalaya is covered with a dense layer of furlike fibers that protect the flowers inside from cold. Insects crawl down a shaft from the top to pollinate the plant.

Animals

Andean Condor

The Andean condor lives where food—small mammals and birds—is scarce. It hunts over a wide territory with a minimum of effort, spreading 3-m (10-ft.)-wide wings to soar for hours on the **updrafts.**

Guanaco

At 3,300 m (11,000 ft.) in Patagonia, the guanaco gets its water by eating grass and leaves. It exposes a thinly furred belly to soak up sun on bright days, and curls up under thick hair on its back when it's cold.

Would You Believe?

More Red Blood Cells

The higher you go above sea level, the less oxygen the air contains. People like this mother and child living in the high Andes of Peru have physically adapted to this "thin air" environment. They have larger hearts and greater lung capacities so they can take bigger breaths. Pint for pint, highlanders' blood includes more red cells to carry oxygen. They don't suffer low-oxygen "mountain sickness": the dizzy spells, headache, and nausea that afflict visitors from lower altitudes.

Altitude Zones

Altitude divides the mountains into distinct microclimates. The summit may be snow covered all year, with thin air that supports little life. A few hundred meters (thousand feet) or more below, trees grow in dense **forests** with other plants and animal populations, such as the grizzly bear at right. Below the forests lie lush valleys sheltered between ridges. The valleys provide fields and pasture for farmers. Some animals and people move up and down the mountain with the changing seasons.

Alpine Butterflies

Lowland butterflies complete their life cycles within a single year. Eggs hatch into caterpillars that eat and grow, splitting their skin several times until they are mature enough to spin cocoons, then change into flying adults. But mountain summers are so short that alpine butterflies need three years' growing time for the same process.

3rd Year

1st Year

2nd Year

Earth ALERT!

Trashing the Mountains

As mountain tourism becomes more popular, mountain ecology suffers. Vehicle and foot traffic break down fragile mountain soils. A single footstep causes so much damage it may take the soil 50 years to recover. Climbers leave garbage behind them. Near the summit of Mount Everest, air is so thin that no one has enough energy to carry camping litter or oxygen bottles back down the mountain, or even the bodies of comrades who have died along the trail.

What Is the Tundra?

Special Landforms

Tundra is a Russian word meaning "treeless." Indeed, the tundra is an area of marshy plains and mountains found in northern latitudes below the icebound Arctic. The soil is matted with ancient, slowly decaying plant fibers, **saturated** with cold water.

Glaciers left over from the ice ages lie across some tundra mountains; the rocky landscapes below the mountains display telltale signs that the ice once covered them all. The brief summers bring mild warmth and long days, but during the long winters temperatures stay well below freezing for months on end. Few people live on the tundra, but human activity there has been increasing.

Twentieth-century mining and oil drilling have left **toxic** wastes. **Ozone** thinning and drifting **radioactive** particles from nuclear bomb tests have poisoned plants and animals. In addition, global warming may cause dramatic changes in the tundra's ecology.

Polygonal ground *(above)* forms where peaty tundra soil freezes and thaws repeatedly. Water fills cracks in the ground and freezes, and the ice pries the surface apart. Some of these features are 30 m (100 ft.) across. Moraines like the one at left in Canada's Yukon Territory are jumbles of rock left when the glaciers that carried them melted 10,000 years ago. They provide homes for birds and small mammals.

Where in the World?

Tundra

What's Permafrost?

Just below the tundra's surface, the soil is permanently frozen. Heat can melt this layer, called permafrost, making it dangerously unstable. New houses are built with special insulation to keep the foundations cold and to prevent them from sinking into the ground, as this house did in Dawson City, Canada. Once softened, permafrost may never recover. The tire tracks above were made in the 1970s.

Endless Plain

This treeless, rolling landscape is a typical stretch of Alaskan tundra. During the short summer, the otherwise barren land abounds with flowering plants, grasses, and berries as food for wildlife. Streams and pools teem with insects and other creatures.

Tundra Close Up

The climate and landscape of the Arctic tundra resemble conditions found during the ice age some 10,000 years ago. The harsh **environment** of this 7,800,000-sq-km (3,000,000-sq-mi.) region does not support a great diversity of **species,** and many inhabitants of the tundra come only for the warm season—but they come in vast numbers!

Insects breed everywhere in the bogs and damp soil. Caribou and moose stream in from the south before the snow is gone. So many birds compete for nest space in early spring that geese raise their broods dangerously close to **predators** like hawks and owls. Isolated from human disturbance, with bountiful food resources and 24 hours of daylight, animals reproduce quickly, build up fat reserves, and leave before winter comes. Year-round plant and animal residents have adapted to extremes in cold, light, and wind. Most have ground-hugging bodies and are covered in dark fur or feathers that absorb sunlight.

Plant Life

Arctic Poppies

Dwarf Willow

Arctic poppies *(right)* flourish in the microclimate created by a muskox bone. The bone soaks up and then radiates the heat of the sun. It shields the plants from wind, and as it decomposes, it enriches the soil. Poppy blossoms follow the path of the sun throughout the day. Insects feed inside, improving the plant's reproduction chances when they fly out dusted with pollen. The dwarf willow *(right),* standing only 12 cm (5 in.) tall, sends out long branches growing along the ground. By lying low, the tree avoids most of the damaging winds.

Caribou

In summer, caribou move north to the tundra from their southern feeding grounds. Some travel more than 1,600 km (1,000 mi.), led by pregnant, antlered females. The adults and newborn calves graze on sedges, blueberries, willow shrubs, lichens, and even mushrooms. In autumn they drift south again to the forested taiga. A caribou herd may number more than 100,000 animals.

Migrants

The tundra is virtually empty in the winter, but temporary residents flock to fill it as the snow melts and days lengthen. Insect swarms attract more than 100 bird species to spend the summer there feeding and breeding. Songbirds feast on insects, and in turn eagles, merlins, and falcons swoop down on the songbirds. Arctic terns are the long-distance champions, flying 20,000 km (12,500 mi.) from the Antarctic to spend three short months in the Arctic, feeding their chicks on fish plucked from shallow waters. Then they head back to the Southern Hemisphere. Many ducks, loons, and geese nest in summer homes in marshes. Among them are brants *(left)*, small geese that feed on water plants and nest near the coast. Once endangered, brant **populations** are now increasing.

Arctic Tern

Brant

Would **You** *Believe?*

The Tall Tale of the Lemmings

It's just a myth that mobs of lemmings—small rodents—throw themselves off cliffs in huge numbers to drown in the sea. Lemming populations do decline suddenly, though. And lemmings do scurry around wildly and sometimes fall off cliffs when crowded and hungry!

Let's **Compare**

Permanent Residents

A few hardy creatures spend the winter on the tundra. Musk-oxen scrape the snow to find grass. They stay warm under dense insulating pelts; their outer hairs are up to 50 cm (20 in.) long. Ground squirrels hibernate in burrows sealed with a plug of earth. The ptarmigan, a grouse, browses on berries and shrubs under the snow. Its compact body retains fat and energy efficiently, and its feet are feather covered for warmth.

Summer Coat

Dressed in gray or tan summer colors to blend in with tundra grasses, the Arctic fox goes after anything edible: lemmings, mice, eggs, birds, and berries. Toward the end of the season, the foxes begin to store food, hiding carcasses of **prey** under rocks.

Winter Coat

Bushy tail, small ears, short legs, and fur on the pads of its feet keep the Arctic fox warm in winter. It grows a white coat to hide against the snow. Foxes hunt hare and ptarmigan, or catch lemmings by listening for them tunneling under the snow, then pouncing through the frozen crust.

Polar Regions Arctic

The polar regions at each end of the earth's axis are alike in some ways and very different in others. The tilt of the axis brings extremely cold winter darkness as well as long summer daylight hours to both the North and the South Poles. Both are permanently covered with ice and snow, but the surrounding oceans teem with many varieties of **marine** life.

There is no landmass around the North Pole, only frozen water. The Arctic Ocean is separated from other oceans by the landmasses of Asia and North America, which limit currents and marine animal migration. The North Polar icecap stays about the same size all year long, though its fringes melt during the brief summer, breaking off as icebergs. The region is blanketed by new snow every year and is influenced by warm and cold winds from nearby Canada, Greenland, and Siberia.

Unlike the South Polar region, the Arctic has a permanent native human **population** living around its edges. Called the Inuit, they have adapted over many centuries to its extreme climatic conditions.

Where in the World?

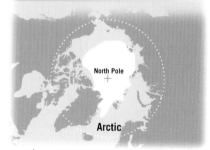

North Pole
+

Arctic

Fast FACTS

Area
Arctic Ocean: 12,260,000 sq km
(4,734,000 sq mi.)

Antarctica: 13,209,000 sq km
(5,100,400 sq mi.)

Coldest Recorded Temperatures
Arctic: -67.7°C (-89.9°F)
Antarctic: -89°C (-128.6°F)

Normal High Temperatures
Arctic: 20°C (68°F)
Antarctic: -15°C (5°F)

Largest Resident Land Animal
Arctic: Polar bear—roughly 2 m
(7 ft.) from nose to tail

Antarctic: Springtail—
12 mm (0.5 in.) long

Bearing the Cold

About 20,000 polar bears live on the Arctic ice, hunting for seals, walrus, and fish. Their webbed toes help them swim well, and hair on the soles of their feet keeps them warm. Polar bears grow dense, waterproof undercoats; their outer coats have hollow guard hairs that trap any warm air.

Arctic Seals

Born and bred on the ice pack, seals like this hooded seal mother and pup can regulate their blood flow and store **oxygen** supplies in their bodies while swimming in the frigid water. Baby seals grow very fast. The hooded seal pups gain about 7 kg (15 lb.) a day during the four to five days that they are nursing.

People in the Arctic

Driving on Ice

An Inuit rescues his huskies from a crack in the softened ice *(above)*. For centuries, Arctic travelers have used dogsleds for transportation. Since the 1950s, snowmobiles have been taking over. Some people, though, continue to prefer dogs. They are cheaper to buy and don't break down easily. And as one Inuit pointed out, in case of emergency "you can't eat your snowmobile."

Earth ALERT

Arctic Pollution

Oil spills from tankers have killed wildlife and disrupted food chains. Global warming softens fringe ice, allowing more icebreakers *(below)* and submarines into Arctic waters; their fuel leaks are **toxic.**

Would YOU Believe?

No Veggies Here!

An Inuit woman slices fish with an ulu. With plants scarce, Inuit once lived on fish, meat, and blubber. Today they battle health problems caused by adding sugar and **carbohydrates** to their diet.

Walruses

Walruses are social animals that live in groups of up to 100 amid the ice along the Arctic shores. The massive adults can weigh 0.9 t (1 tn.) or more. Both males and females grow tusks, which they use to hoist themselves up onto land. Rooting about on the seafloor with their snouts, walruses suck clams out of their shells, eating thousands of clams per day. To attract mates, males bellow song sequences that carry for a mile or more underwater.

Antarctica

t the southern end of the earth's axis, Antarctica presents a fascinating **environment** to scientists who study it. In contrast to the watery Arctic, this continent is a landmass of high, rocky mountains, covered with ice and snow, yet so dry that it is classed as a desert. The frozen expanse of Antarctica holds more than 70 percent of the world's fresh water in the form of ice. But little new precipitation falls; blizzards that howl across the land are blowing ancient snow. Millions of years ago Antarctica lay near the **equator** and enjoyed a warm climate. Fossils of tropical plants, oil, and mineral deposits have been found in the rocks. Though the Arctic has been home to humans for thousands of years, the Antarctic has been empty: The first people to live there through an entire year came in 1899. Even today there is no permanent **population;** research bases host hundreds of temporary residents. Generators, trash dumps, and construction supporting the bases have brought pollution to the Antarctic. New rules enforced by several countries aim to limit future damage.

Antarctica

Ross Ice Shelf

his block of ice looms up nearly 75 m (250 ft.) above the sea and reaches down to 250 m (800 ft.) below the surface for hundreds of miles around the coast. Its mass ensures constant cold air across the land. Sections that drop off into the sea form icebergs the size of small countries, influencing conditions far out to sea.

Mountains under Ice

erched high on a nunatak, the exposed peak of a buried mountain range, a scientist scans for microscopic life forms—the largest inhabitants of this frigid environment! The illustration below shows how deep the Antarctic icecap lies across the mountains: Ice at the base froze there 200,000 years ago. Only 2 percent of the continent is exposed rock.

Descent into the Deep

Scientists climb into an ice cave to explore the edge of a volcanic crater. Mount Erebus, an active volcano, simmers on the Ross Ice Shelf. **Glaciers** lie undisturbed in sub-zero temperatures on the slopes as liquid magma bubbles and smokes red hot in the caldera below. The melted ice at the rim creates a **habitat** for **algae** and **bacteria**.

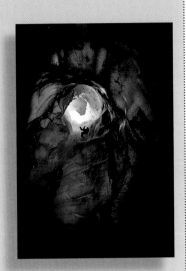

Research Stations

Antarctica is being analyzed by scientists from some 30 research stations. Those below probe the origins of the universe in an experiment near absolute zero, the coldest temperature. Each year about 3,000 researchers here use computers and other space-age equipment to study geologic history, ice sheets, meteorites, **ozone** layer, wildlife cycles, and ocean life.

I Was There!

In 1915 the ship *Endurance* (above) was caught in pack ice near Antarctica, trapping British explorer Ernest Shackleton and 27 companions.

"Mighty blocks of ice, gripped between meeting floes, rose slowly until they jumped like cherrystones squeezed between thumb and finger . . . we can do nothing until the ice releases our ship. In the meantime, the pressure continues, and it is hard to foresee the outcome," wrote Shackleton.

Ten months later the ship was crushed; all the men were rescued after 19 months on the ice.

Antarctica Close up

P lants, insects, fish, birds, and even a few
mammals call Antarctica home—at least for
part of the year. The seasons rule their behavior,
and the creatures have adapted to the feast-or-
famine conditions imposed by the extremes of climate.

The permanent land-based life forms are tiny and
nearly invisible: **algae,** mosses, **bacteria,** red mites, and
springtails *(opposite)*. The birds and mammals migrate,
shuttling between breeding sites on the continent and
the surrounding fish-filled waters, where they feed to
regain their strength.

In the ocean north of Antarctica, frigid and warmer
water mix in a zone about 40 km (25 mi.) wide called
the Antarctic Convergence. Currents and temperatures
change there, as does the chemistry of the water, in
which grow masses of algae and plankton that form the
base of Antarctica's food chain. In complete contrast to
the desolate land, this is one of the richest biological
regions on earth. Billions of krill and fish flourish on
this diet of algae and plankton and in turn serve as **prey**
for penguins, albatrosses, seals, and whales.

Flight Underwater

P enguins cannot fly, but underwater they take wing. Unlike
other water birds that paddle with
their feet, penguins use only their
wings for propulsion, in effect
flying through the water as other
birds do in the air. Some of the
17 **species,** such as the king
penguins at right, spend up to
three-quarters of their life in the
water, feasting on the ocean's
food supply. They come ashore
only to breed and raise their chicks.

Paltry Plant Life

Mosses

Mosses grow in dense clumps on the rocky shores of islands within the Antarctic Circle. The brilliant green top layers contain chlorophyll for photosynthesis. Lower layers are brown.

Algae

It's not Saint Patrick's Day—this snow is colored with algae! Single-celled algae bloom in greens, reds, and yellows on sloping snowfields when rare thaws melt the surface slightly.

Lichens

Lichens, composed of an alga and fungus living mutualistically, grow wherever they can find nutrients. Lichens do especially well near seabird nesting sites, fertilized by the birds' droppings.

What's an Extremophile?

The springtail *(above)* is a tiny wingless insect found in vast numbers worldwide. Antarctic springtails are extremophiles—creatures that have adapted to life in an extreme **environment**. They are the only insects that live independently in the frozen interior of the continent. They can drop their body temperature to below -30°C (-22°F), and they will survive for up to a month encased in ice.

Cool Critters

Seals

Several seal species, including fur seals like this mother and pup, visit Antarctic shores to feed on penguins, krill, and fish. Weddell seals sing special songs to mark their territories around the breathing holes they gnaw through the ice. Crabeaters live in the ice pack and eat mostly krill, not crabs. There are more crabeater seals—50 million—than any other large mammal in the world after humans!

Krill

Tiny, shrimplike krill are the center of the Antarctic food chain. They excrete nitrogen, which fertilizes the floating plants the krill themselves eat. Whales, seals, birds, and fish, in turn, feed on the krill. These crustaceans, which can live up to 40 years, swim in huge schools with all the bodies aligned. Krill communicate with chemical light flashes.

Birds

The rocky Antarctic Peninsula and the islands to its north are the nurseries for millions of seabirds each summer. Penguins, terns, petrels, skuas, and albatrosses form colonies there. The wandering albatross *(left)* is the largest seabird in the world, with a wingspan of more than 3.5 m (11 ft.). Albatrosses can soar on the wind for many hours without flapping and fly at speeds of up to 80 km/h (50 mph).

Special Habitats

When natural barriers such as mountain chains or oceans isolate an area of land, that area often becomes a special **habitat.** On many islands, for example, the plants and animals have been separated from all other **species** for a very long time. As a result, they may have evolved differently, becoming unique species that cannot be found anywhere else in the world.

Such odd **communities** of flora and fauna are valuable to the world's **biodiversity.** They are also vulnerable to the introduction of species from other places. Most are defenseless against new **predators** and competitors. Conservationists struggle to protect the unusual plants and animals found in these places set apart from the rest of the world. When you see some of the strange and intriguing life forms special habitats produce, you'll understand why they're protected.

Hot Spots

Hawaii

Galápagos

Papua New Guinea

Madagascar

Australia

New Zealand

Biodiversity hot spots are small areas in the world where rare species have developed. Many of the plants and animals in these places can't be found anywhere else. The map above shows the locations of the hot spot special habitats featured on these pages.

New Guinea

Looking as if it has just stepped out of a beauty salon, the Victoria crowned pigeon shows off its brilliant colors. About 700 known bird species call New Guinea, the world's second-largest island, home. That's more than the total number of bird species in all of Europe. Scientists know that many more species that have not yet been discovered reside in the dense rain forests of the island.

Galápagos

Among the many strange animals found on the volcanic islands that make up the Galápagos are 270-kg (600-lb.) giant tortoises *(above)* and the world's only **marine** iguanas *(left)*. The iguanas are specially equipped with glands that remove salt from seawater. The lizards then "sneeze" out the salt through their nostrils.

Hawaii

Before pigs, goats, deer, and other plant eaters were introduced to Hawaii, there were no browsing mammals. Free from predators, Hawaii's plants, like these lobelias and greenswords, evolved without protective thorns or toxins. Today they are defenseless against many nonnative animals that eat them.

New Zealand

What do kakapos *(above)*, kiwis, takahes, and wekas have in common? They are all birds that can't fly. A wide variety of flightless bird species evolved in New Zealand because there were no mammals to hunt them. Now, because of cats, dogs, and other invaders humans brought to the country, only these four species of flightless birds still exist. Even they are seriously **endangered**.

Australia

Isolated from the rest of the world for 40 million years, Australia has produced a lot of odd animals that can't be found anywhere else. The country is well known for its variety of marsupials, but it also supports 2,830 unique plant species and 765 reptile species (more than any other country), 90 percent of which are unique to Australia.

Kangaroos

Most marsupials, like this female kangaroo, are found in Australia. Marsupials nourish their young in an abdominal pouch; other mammals do so in a womb.

Thorny Devil

This well-armored lizard looks fiercely menacing. It is only several centimeters long and moves sluggishly.

Madagascar Close up

Desert Trees

eople often call Madagascar the land that time forgot. The 1,600-km (1,000-mi.)-long island separated from Africa's mainland about 165 million years ago. Since then, its plants and animals have evolved in isolation, and many of them exist nowhere else in the world. Some may not even have been discovered yet by scientists.

Madagascar is where the lemur (a monkeylike animal) lives, and at least half of the world's **species** of chameleons. More than half of Madagascar's 10,000 known species of flowering plants are unique to this **environment.** Of the 300 or so known reptile species, 95 percent are found only on this island. Some of these plants and animals look decidedly weird, as you can see on these pages. Such diversity is possible in part because Madagascar's **ecosystems** include tropical **forests**, deserts, and **temperate** regions.

Bottle Tree

In the desert regions of Madagascar, trees have special ways to survive extremely dry conditions. The bottle tree *Moringa drouhardii*, for example, has a gray, bulbous trunk in which water is stored. It looks similar to the baobab trees in Africa, India, and Australia but is actually a different species.

Octopus Tree

Like the bottle tree, the octopus tree survives in Madagascar's dry regions because it is able to store water. The green leaves that cover the tree are well protected from thirsty **predators** by long, sharp spines that also cover the trunk and branches.

Flower Cure

he pink-petaled rosy periwinkle held by a Malagasy girl is not just a pretty flower. The plant contains a chemical that can stop childhood leukemia, a type of cancer. In the 1960s, only 20 percent of children with leukemia recovered. Now, in large part because of the medicine derived from Madagascar's periwinkle, there is a 99 percent chance of remission.

Of the thousands of other plants growing in Madagascar, many of them have not been studied by scientists yet. It may turn out that they, too, are sources of important medicines or have other good uses.

Fearsome Fossa

adagascar's largest carnivore is the fossa, an animal that looks like a small cougar. The sleek hunter eats small mammals, including lemurs, and birds primarily, but it also dines on reptiles, frogs, and insects. The fossa's powerful tail is as long as its body; it uses the tail for support by wrapping it around branches when climbing trees, where it often finds its meals.

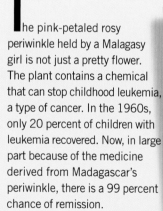

Leaping Lemurs

Ring-Tailed Mongoose

The ring-tailed mongoose is one of four mongoose species on Madagascar. The animal scours the trees and the ground for snails, eggs, insects, reptiles, and small lemurs to eat. Legend says that if hikers see two of these creatures wrestling in the forest, they should not laugh out loud or they will become lost forever.

How Big?

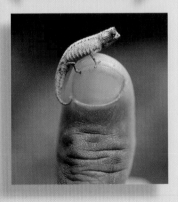

Little Lizard

Half of the world's species of chameleons are found in Madagascar. The smallest are part of the **genus** *Brookesia* and can be less than 25 mm (1 in.) long.

The more than two dozen species of lemurs on Madagascar come in all shapes and sizes. Most are cute, like these sifakas perched in a tree. They are named for the sound they make when alarmed while on the ground: *shifakh!* There's a different alarm call when they are in trees. Less cuddly is the black-and-silver aye-aye *(above)*, a creature so bizarre looking it took scientists almost a century to agree that it's a lemur. It uses its bony middle finger to scrape insects out of tree bark.

A World of Resources

A t first glance, our planet's **natural resources** seem as though they could last forever. Rivers crowded with fish flow across every continent, and trees of all kinds—from hardy spruces in cold climates to tall teak trees in tropical rain forests—blanket the globe. Below the surface the earth's interior is just as rich with **fossil fuels**—oil, coal, and natural gas—that provide about 90 percent of our energy.

These fuels were formed from long-dead plants that were subjected to high pressures and temperatures for millions of years. There are an estimated 9.9 trillion t (11 trillion tn.) of coal in the earth and two thousand trillion barrels of oil. This seems like a huge amount, but about 30 percent of all the earth's oil has already been burned. And as the world's **population** grows, so does the demand. Once natural resources, such as coal and oil, are used up, they cannot be replenished. Scientists are working hard to invent alternative fuels.

WATER

Water—The Gift of Life

The green circles on the eastern Colorado prairie *(above)* are potato and barley fields watered by rotating sprinklers. Many dry areas can be farmed only if water is brought from far away—a process known as irrigation.

COAL

Coal Mining

A huge shovel loads coal from a strip mine in Wyoming. Open-air mines like this strip all vegetation and topsoil from the surface of the land to get to the underlying coal. These mines are devastating to the **environment** because nothing can grow there for years afterward.

What Are Our Natural Resources?

TIMBER

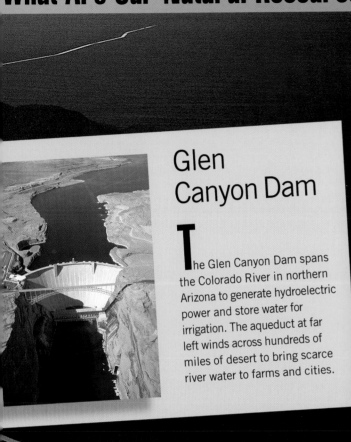

Glen Canyon Dam

The Glen Canyon Dam spans the Colorado River in northern Arizona to generate hydroelectric power and store water for irrigation. The aqueduct at far left winds across hundreds of miles of desert to bring scarce river water to farms and cities.

Trees—A Renewable Resource

Vast forests like this one in Sweden provide the world's wood and paper. Unlike oil and gas, trees are a renewable resource—we can grow more, provided we **preserve** enough forests and don't cut down too many trees at once.

Our Thirst for Oil

In the United States alone, some 17 million barrels of oil are consumed every day. More than half of that total is burned in vehicles like cars and trucks and used for heating oil. And the demand for oil is constantly going up. According to some estimates, the number of miles driven by Americans will double by 2020. Many scientists are looking for ways to make our vehicles more energy efficient, so they can travel farther on the same amount of gasoline.

OIL

Offshore Oil Rigs

Oil reserves under dry land have become harder to find, so rigs like the one above have begun drilling for oil offshore.

Oil Refineries

Oil refineries convert crude oil straight from the well into products like gasoline, diesel fuel, kerosene, and heating oil.

Would **You** Believe?

Fresh Water

Less than one-half of 1 percent of all the water on earth is drinkable. If all the earth's water could fit in a 4-l (1-gal.) jar, the amount of fresh water would barely fill a tablespoon.

Resources Close up

Our planet's human **population** is growing so fast that our sources of energy and **natural resources** may not be sufficient a century from now. For example, scientists believe that nearly 80 percent of the earth's oil reserves have already been found.

But even if today's energy sources hold out, we must still deal with the pollution they produce. The burning of **fossil fuels**—oil, coal, and natural gas—throws huge amounts of **pollutants** into the atmosphere, where they poison the air we breathe and create hazards like **acid rain** (*page* 102). Accidents can also do great damage to the **environment.** Every year oil spills dump an average of 0.9 million t (1 million tn.) of oil into the world's oceans.

For these reasons, many people are searching for alternatives to fossil fuels. Some solutions, like electric cars, are already in the experimental stage. In fact, California passed a law requiring that 10 percent of all new cars in the state must be pollution free by the year 2003.

Increased Strain on the Land

New developments in the desert, like this one in Las Vegas, Nevada, spell disaster for the area's native plants and animals. Suburban expansion also increases the demand for water, lumber, and energy. What's worse, the cars that are needed to get around this community contribute to air pollution.

Vanishing Forests

Logging
With increasing demand for wood products, many countries feel the pressure to open more of their forests to logging. The logging not only reduces the forests themselves, but it can also create **erosion** that harms the surrounding land and nearby bodies of water.

Deforestation
Every second, an area of rain forest the size of one and a half football fields is burned to create new farmland. Beyond destroying a valuable **ecosystem,** the burning also produces harmful amounts of **carbon dioxide,** which contributes to the greenhouse effect (*pages* 28-29).

Problems with Oil

The Energy Crisis
In the early 1970s, many Middle Eastern countries stopped selling their oil to the United States. The resulting shortage of gasoline created long lines at gas stations (*left*) and pointed out the danger of relying on dwindling supplies of oil for energy.

Oil Spills
In 1989, the oil tanker *Exxon Valdez* ran aground in Alaska, spilling more than 11 million barrels of oil. Hundreds of miles of shoreline were contaminated, and thousands of birds like this cormorant were injured or killed by the oil. The cleanup continues to this day.

Energy Alternatives

Wind Energy

The strong winds at California's Altamont Pass *(above)* generate a lot of wind energy. The 17,000 wind generators throughout the state provide enough electricity for all the homes in San Francisco.

Solar Power

Solar heat collectors on the roofs of many California towns generate clean electricity. In places like the American West, where sunlight is plentiful year round, solar power is an ideal alternative energy source.

Nuclear Hazards

The risks of **nuclear energy** were made clear in 1979 when a minor accident at the Three Mile Island nuclear power plant in Pennsylvania sent a small amount of **radiation** into the atmosphere. Seven years later, a far more serious accident at Russia's Chernobyl power station *(left)* released a huge quantity of radiation. The poisonous cloud quickly spread across Europe and contaminated millions of acres of farms and forests. Thirty-two people died immediately, and thousands more have radiation-induced illnesses.

Would You Believe?

The new car called Impact *(below)* runs on electricity rather than gas and produces no pollution. This model can travel only about 88 km (55 mi.) before its battery needs to be recharged. Most major car-makers are working on electric cars that will be able to travel farther between recharges.

An Electric Car

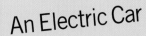

Trashing Our Home

The land on which we all depend for life is being polluted every day in a number of ways. In the industrialized nations of North America and Europe, for example, every family produces an average of 0.9 t (1 tn.) of trash every year. An obvious solution is to make less garbage and find better ways of handling what is left. Recycling reduces the amount of trash that goes into **landfills** and also saves energy. It takes less energy to **recycle** an object such as an aluminum can, for example, than to produce it from scratch.

The **fertilizers** and **pesticides** used by farmers and homeowners are another source of pollution. These poisonous chemicals seep into the ground, where they can remain for years or be washed into the water supply. Either way, they pose a deadly hazard to plants, animals, and people. It is important to find new ways to protect crops and the earth.

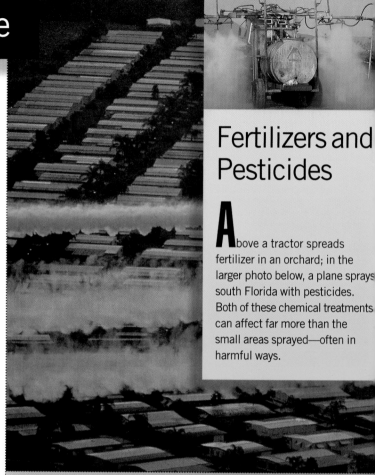

Fertilizers and Pesticides

Above a tractor spreads fertilizer in an orchard; in the larger photo below, a plane sprays south Florida with pesticides. Both of these chemical treatments can affect far more than the small areas sprayed—often in harmful ways.

People — Rachel Carson

American naturalist Rachel Carson (1907-1964) helped stir the public to environmental action with her 1962 book *Silent Spring.* Carson described in great detail the damage that had been caused by the widespread use of pesticides in the 1940s and 1950s. The chemicals, as it turned out, killed not only the targeted insects but also animals that ate the insects, and so on up the food chain. As a result, birds like the bald eagle, near the top of the food chain, were being poisoned.

The Problem with Garbage

Landfills

One of the most common ways to dispose of garbage is by sending it to a landfill *(above)*, where it is spread out and crushed by bulldozers, treated with chemicals, and then covered with dirt. Burying garbage, however, doesn't solve the problem. People produce so much trash that landfills are running out of space, and the landfills themselves create environmental hazards when **pollutants** leak into the surrounding soil.

Soil Erosion

When entire forests are cut down, the underlying soil tends to wash away, or **erode.** This destroys the ability of a forest to renew itself and can also clog rivers and lakes, wiping out **aquatic** species that need clear, fast-moving water to survive.

Animal Farms

Large poultry and hog farms consume a lot of resources and can also harm the environment. Every year they produce tons of waste, which can seep into the soil and water. It takes 3.5 kg (7 lb.) of feed to raise 0.5 kg (1 lb.) of pork, and 1.5 kg (3 lb.) of feed to produce one chicken egg.

Recycling

Three workers survey a towering wall of crushed aluminum cans at a Tennessee recycling plant. The energy saved by recycling just 10 aluminum cans is the equivalent of about half a tank of gasoline. Multiplied by millions, the savings become a big help to the **environment.**

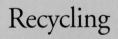

Would **You** *Believe?*

Wearing Plastic

One way to recycle plastic is to melt it down and spin it into clothing fibers. It takes 25 clear 1-l (33.8-oz.) bottles to weave enough fabric for one Polartec® jacket.

Pollution in the Air

Effects of Air Pollution

The air around us can be polluted in many ways, and not all of them are visible to the naked eye. Most people associate air pollution with **smog,** the brown haze that often blankets large cities (*far right*) and can trigger breathing problems in people who live with it every day.

One hazard not immediately visible is **acid rain.** Car and factory **emissions** contain nitrogen and sulfur, which combine with water in the air to form nitric and sulfuric acids. These **corrosive** liquids fall to earth when it rains. Acid rain is responsible for killing coniferous forests at high elevations and poisoning lakes in much of Europe and North America.

A further danger from air pollution is damage to the earth's ozone layer. Another class of chemicals released into the atmosphere interferes with a form of **oxygen** called **ozone,** which protects the earth from much of the harmful effect of the sun's rays.

Acid Rain

The barren trees at left are victims of acid rain. Scientists estimate that more than half the forests in Germany, Norway, and eastern Europe have been damaged by acid rain. Forests in the eastern U.S. and Canada have also been seriously affected.

Pollution Masks

In heavily polluted cities like Kuala Lumpur, Malaysia, people who spend long periods of time outdoors sometimes don masks that filter out soot and smoke from the air. Most of this **urban** pollution comes from automobile exhaust.

The Growing Ozone Hole

The earth is blanketed with a layer of ozone molecules, which consist of three oxygen atoms bound together. The ozone layer serves a vital purpose: It blocks much of the **ultraviolet radiation** from the sun. In small doses ultraviolet radiation produces suntans, but in larger amounts it can cause skin cancer and even blindness.

In the mid-1980s, scientists discovered that the ozone layer over the South Pole was starting to thin. The diagram at right shows growth in the ozone hole over the course of a decade and a half; orange and yellow areas show high concentrations of ozone, whereas purple areas represent depleted ozone.

Much of the blame was placed on chemicals called chlorofluorocarbons (CFCs), which interfere with ozone formation in the atmosphere. A major source of CFCs is **aerosol** cans. Many countries have taken steps to reduce CFC emissions —such as banning aerosol cans —but the effects of CFCs already in the air may take many years to go away.

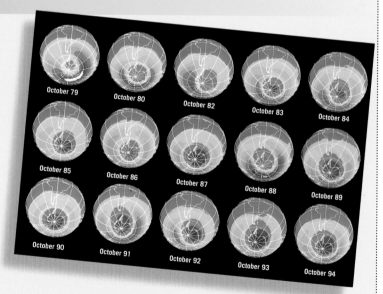

October 79 · October 80 · October 82 · October 83 · October 84
October 85 · October 86 · October 87 · October 88 · October 89
October 90 · October 91 · October 92 · October 93 · October 94

Bad Air Days

A SMOGGY DAY

A CLEAR DAY

The Faces of Los Angeles

With millions of cars, Los Angeles is one of America's most polluted cities. Changes in the weather can greatly alter the air quality in the city. On days like the one at left, people are advised to spend as little time as possible outdoors.

Protecting the Water

Rebirth of a River

In the past, people treated our planet's water supply as though it were limitless. Now, as industrial output and **population** growth continue to damage the quality of the water around us, it has become clear that we are in danger of running out of clean water.

Even today, some factories in parts of the world routinely dump **pollutants** directly into rivers and oceans, killing **aquatic** life and posing a health hazard to people. As a result, it is no longer safe to fish or swim in many lakes and rivers around the world. Many countries have taken steps to control or eliminate water pollutants, though much remains to be done. In the United States, the Environmental Protection Agency helps enforce laws like the Clean Water Acts that protect American waterways. But many developing countries lag far behind in protecting their waters.

BEFORE

In the 1960s, pollution and dye from a local paper mill turned the Nashua River in Massachusetts into a **toxic** mess. Fumes from the river were so toxic that they corroded the paint on buildings.

Holes in the Ground

Where fresh surface water is in short supply, deep wells can make up the difference. But when too much underground water is pumped to the surface, the soil below can become unstable. Large sections of land may then collapse, forming so-called sinkholes. The sinkhole below developed in Winter Park, Florida.

Would You Believe?

Rivers of Fire

It may sound impossible, but rivers can become so polluted with flammable substances that they actually catch fire. The most famous example took place in 1969 when a blaze broke out on the Cuyahoga River in Cleveland, Ohio. This embarrassment spurred local residents to organize a cleanup campaign.

Sewage in the Water

In many developing countries, raw **sewage** receives little or no treatment before it reaches the public water supply. At right, sewage washes into a canal that runs through the slums of Belize City in the Central American country of Belize. Untreated water contains countless disease-causing organisms and poses a severe health problem in developing countries around the world. In fact, poor sanitation is a major cause of disease and death for more than a third of the world's population.

After a decades-long cleanup effort, the Nashua River and its tributaries run far cleaner. The rivers are now prime fishing grounds, and a magnet for canoeists and swimmers.

Algae Blooms

Tiny aquatic organisms called **algae** feed on **fertilizers** and other pollutants that run into lakes and streams. This excess food supply causes their population to soar, resulting in a so-called algae bloom. Sometimes the algae turn the water red, causing a red tide *(below)*. Algae blooms are harmful because they use up much of the **oxygen** dissolved in the water, leaving less oxygen for other aquatic life. Large algae blooms can suffocate millions of fish.

Hazardous Runoff

Water stained by dissolved iron rushes from an outlet pipe in a Colorado mine. Though this runoff will be treated before it meets the general water supply, contaminated water from many old abandoned mines still seeps directly into the **ground water.** And many factories release clean runoff that is hotter than the surrounding water, killing fish and other aquatic life in the process.

Alien Species

When a plant or an animal finds its way to an **environment** where it never lived before, scientists call it an exotic, or alien, **species.** Sometimes species are brought to a new place on purpose, to be hunted for food or to prey on other species that are considered pests. But plants and animals can also "hitchhike" to new homes in a variety of ways. Travelers may accidentally carry seeds or insects along when they fly from one country or continent to another. Animals can hide unnoticed on planes or ships and then get off wherever the vessel stops.

Alien species often grow and reproduce rapidly because they usually have no natural **predators** in their new location. They can crowd out native species, either by preying on them or by taking over food resources and living space. Once an alien species establishes itself in a new **habitat,** it may turn into a pest itself, and it is practically impossible to get rid of.

A Vine Mess

Like something out of a horror movie, a vine called kudzu has taken over the eastern United States *(orange on map)*. In the early 1930s, the government paid farmers to plant the Japanese vine to control soil **erosion.** It worked too well, though: The hardy weed can grow 0.3 m (1 ft.) a day.

How Many?

"Musseling" In

Lake Erie has been invaded by freshwater mollusks called zebra mussels. These natives of Asia arrived in the mid-1980s, probably aboard a ship from Europe. Since then, they have multiplied, clogging water pipes and littering beaches. In some places millions of zebra mussels carpet the lake bottom! So far, scientists have found no way to prevent them from spreading into other lakes and rivers.

Snakes Alive!

The western Pacific island of Guam has been invaded by aliens with bulging eyes and legless bodies up to 3 m (10 ft.) long: They are brown tree snakes *(left)*. Since arriving as stowaways on military ships after World War II, the snakes have multiplied into the millions. The mildly poisonous snakes have wiped out nine of 12 native **forest** birds and have even been known to snatch pets from backyards.

Marauding Mongoose

Mongooses—the snake- and rodent-fighting mammals of India—were imported to Hawaii to prey on rats overrunning sugarcane fields. But the plan backfired. Mongooses hunt only during the day, whereas the rats come out at night. So instead of controlling pests, mongooses eat ground-nesting birds, including Hawaii's endangered state bird, the nene.

Earth ALERT!

Attack from Within

Hardwood trees in America are being attacked by a bug that invaded the country, probably in wooden packing crates from China. The long-horned beetle eats the insides of trees until they weaken and die. The only way to keep the bugs from spreading is to cut down and destroy any trees they infest.

Sniffing Out Intruders

International airports around the world have specially trained dogs—usually beagles—that sniff passengers and bags for fruits, meats, and other foods that can carry pests and diseases. They also keep a nose out for live snakes and birds that are imported illegally.

Urban Wildlife

Human **populations** have taken over many of the world's wild places. As a result, wild animals come into contact with ever growing cities more often. Some creatures have successfully made new homes in these urban **environments.** Rock doves that nest on cliffs by the sea have evolved into the common pigeons found on building ledges in cities all over the world. Hawks and other birds of prey can be found nesting near the tops of skyscrapers in New York.

Raccoons and skunks invade city trash dumps at night in search of discarded food. And in the **tropics,** lizards have settled comfortably among the city folk. Many of these **species** have adapted to city life so well that they are now considered pests by their human neighbors.

Some wild animals will never be city dwellers. For them, it's especially important to establish parks and wildlife reserves where they can live undisturbed by human activity.

Monkey Mugger

Across southern Asia, macaque monkeys have made themselves at home in cities. They swing from power lines *(right)* as though they were tree branches. And the furry criminals have learned the art of robbery, stealing everything from ice-cream cones *(left)* to wallets.

Thieves in the Night

Furry masked bandits can often be found rummaging through trash cans in cities and towns across North America. Raccoons are highly adaptable animals that used to live primarily in the woods. But, having found a constant and easily reachable food supply in people's backyards and alleys, many raccoons now make their homes in sheds and attics.

How Many?

Kingdom of the Crabs

Every spring, a tide of red makes its way across Christmas Island northwest of Australia. More than 100 million red crabs hike from their year-round home in the island's **forests** to the sea, where they breed. During the nine- to 18-day migration, nearly a million crabs die, mostly because of close encounters with **urban** life. Traveling in such huge numbers they get run over by cars as they scuttle across roads. And about 100,000 die each year under the wheels of trains while crossing tracks.

City Fisherman

North America's great blue heron has adapted well to city life. Althoug most still eat fish and shellfish, those who live near urban areas also dine rats, muskrats, gophers, and even kittens. Below, a young heron enjoys a meal from a backyard fishpond.

Monkeying Around

Life at the Edge

A group of giraffes browse in a national park in the East African nation of Kenya. On the horizon behind them lies the skyline of Nairobi, Kenya's fast growing capital. As the city expands, it eats up more and more land that giraffes, the world's tallest animals, used to call home.

Endangered Species

What is an **endangered** species? A **species** is called endangered when its total **population** becomes so small that it may soon vanish from the earth. This applies to plants and animals. Scientists have a long list of such species and are working hard to help **preserve** them.

Plants and animals become endangered for many reasons. The natural process of **evolution** replaces species with stronger and better-adapted versions of themselves. But today species are dying out at an alarming rate. Three-quarters of the world's bird populations are threatened with extinction, as are more than two-thirds of the world's **primates.** And one of every 10 plant species will probably disappear from the planet forever. The two main causes—**habitat** loss and overhunting—are the result of people's actions, not natural evolution.

Gone Forever?

The quagga, a relative of the zebra, once roamed the plains of Africa in huge herds. But hunters killed so many for their meat and hides that by 1883 they were **extinct.** Scientists in South Africa have started breeding zebras that show some of the physical attributes of the quagga in hopes of bringing it back from extinction.

Mandrill

The brightly colored face of western Africa's mandrill, a large relative of the baboon, is slowly disappearing. Once used in scientific experiments, the mandrill is now hunted for food. Adding to its troubles is the rapid disappearance of its tropical **forest** habitat.

Sun Bear

The sun bear, named for the creamy yellow mark on its chest, is one of the rarest animals on earth. Poaching and logging in the bear's Malayan rain forest habitat have reduced its population to between 600 and 1,000.

Hyacinth Macaw

The South American hyacinth macaw, largest of all parrots, is about 1.2 m (4 ft.) long when fully grown. Habitat destruction and poaching make it unlikely this beautiful bird will survive in the wild.

Fragile Frog

Got a frog in your throat? The female gastric-brooding frog does. She incubates her young in her stomach and gives birth through her mouth. First discovered in Australian streams in the 1970s, it may now be extinct.

Babirusa

A large, shy wild pig, the babirusa is fast disappearing from its home on the Indonesian island of Celebes. Its tusks are actually teeth that grow continuously. Eventually, in the male, they pierce the jawbones of the skull.

People | Valmik Thapar

Valmik Thapar saw his first tiger when he was nine years old and decided to devote himself to protecting the endangered species. He teaches local village children about tigers by taking them to a national park in India to see tigers up close. About 100 years ago, 500,000 tigers lived in India alone. Now, fewer than 6,000 are alive in the world.

How Many?

1 Mammal
1 Bird
1 Fish
1 Plant
1 Insect

1   2   4   70   180

Plants and animals are becoming extinct faster now than at any other time in earth's history. According to scientists, for every mammal that becomes extinct, two birds, four to six fish, 70 plants, and 180 insects are also lost. Some scientists suspect that as many as 100 species disappear from the world each day, which is about one every 15 minutes. Many of these plants and animals live in habitats so remote that they are not even identified before they vanish.

Saving Species

People around the world are finding ways to help protect our **endangered** wildlife. Some methods of preservation are highly scientific. Others are simply a response to basic needs, providing a safe **habitat,** food, or medical attention. One approach that has helped some **species** is called captive breeding. In this program, endangered animals mate and have their young in zoos or other controlled **environments.** When they are old enough, the offspring are released into the wild.

Why go to all this trouble to save plants and animals? For one thing, they are part of a natural system that keeps our planet's **ecosystem** in balance. They are also a valuable source of medicines, food, scientific knowledge, and a variety of other useful products. They filter water, control destructive pests, and fill a particular **niche** in their ecosystem. But just as important, the earth's diversity of plants and animals is a source of beauty and pleasure.

Flying High Again

In the 1960s, the bald eagle was nearly **extinct** in the United States. Hunting, loss of habitat, and especially poisoning from the **pesticide** DDT had seriously reduced the species. Eager to save this national symbol, conservationists worked to **preserve** bald eagle habitats. They also bred birds in captivity and released them into the wild. Now there are more than 5,000 nesting pairs in the continental United States, and the bird's status has officially changed from endangered to threatened.

St. Tiggywinkles

If you were a hedgehog with a broken jaw in England, where would you go for help? How about St. Tiggywinkles, the wildlife hospital run by Les and Sue Stocker? Named after a character in a book by Beatrix Potter, the author of the Peter Rabbit stories, the hospital treats about 8,000 injured animals each year.

Stand-In Mom

Would **You** _Believe?_

There's not much family resemblance between this mother and child. That's because the mother was just a substitute. In hopes of increasing the number of endangered mountain zebras, scientists in England implanted the **embryo** of a mountain zebra in the womb of a common pony mare. The surrogate mother carried the developing embryo to full term and gave birth to a healthy zebra foal. Perhaps this kind of strategy can help other species survive, too.

Elephant Orphanage

When **poachers** kill adult elephants, baby elephants are often left behind to die. That's why Daphne Sheldrick turned her home in Nairobi, Kenya, into an orphanage for elephants. Her trained staff lives with the baby giants 24 hours a day, assuming the role of mother. When the elephants are old enough, they are released into a wild herd.

People | Wangari Maathai

Wangari Maathai has resolved to protect the **forests** of Africa. In 1977, she started the Green Belt Movement. Most of its members are women, and together they have planted some 10 million trees in more than a dozen African nations. In addition, Maathai was the first woman in Kenya to earn a Ph.D.—in anatomy—and the first female professor at the University of Nairobi.

Strange But TRUE! | The Future on Ice

A bank in London is making deposits to protect our planet's future. Kew Seed Bank has seeds from about 4,000 plant species—including Africa's mugongo tree *(right)*—that are kept frozen in a -20°C (-4°F) vault. Carefully cleaned of mold and insects before being stored, the seeds are expected to last for several hundred years. By then, we may be able to reintroduce endangered or extinct plants into the wild.

Forming New Habitats

Starting from Scratch

When **glaciers** retreat from an area, they leave behind a lifeless landscape. Gradually, over a period of several hundred years, the land is colonized by plants in a process ecologists call primary succession.

When an existing **ecosystem** is destroyed by a natural disaster such as a forest fire or the 1980 eruption of Mount Saint Helens in Washington State, secondary succession occurs. The soil is still there, so plants establish themselves more quickly than in a primary succession.

Plants called pioneer **species** arrive first when a new **habitat** forms. They have the ability to survive even in harsh soil and climate conditions. These grasses and shrubs produce huge numbers of lightweight seeds that are easily carried by the wind. Pioneer species bind the soil and enrich it with **nutrients** so other less hardy species can take root.

As a glacier melts, it exposes barren rubble that has been covered by ice for perhaps thousands of years. Over time, **fertile** soil is created by mosses and lichens that grow and then decay, paving the way for other species *(photos below)*.

After the Glacier

5-35 Years

Dryas drummondii (below), a rugged plant with a yellow flower, is typically the next species to take root in large numbers. It spreads out over the barren ground in a low, dense mat.

70-200 Years

Shade-tolerant hemlocks are the last on the scene. They are able to grow beneath the spruce trees and eventually overtake them in height.

0-5 Years

Greenish gray mosses are the first plants to take root, wherever a bit of soil has blown in or, as here, on top of moose droppings. They form a network of clumps, anchoring soil for the next species.

35-70 Years

Low-growing alders crowd out the dryas, followed by taller cottonwoods *(above)*. Next the spruces appear, reproducing with seeds and by extending roots from low branches.

Wiping Out an Ecosystem

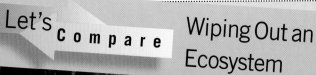

BEFORE

Before the eruption of Mount Saint Helens, Venus Lake teemed with life. Tall fir trees and lush greenery surrounded the beautiful lake.

AFTER

The eruption decimated Venus Lake's ecosystem, making the area hard to recognize. But nature will find a way to recover.

Recovering from a Disaster

A habitat devastated by a natural disaster such as a flood, fire, or volcanic eruption still contains evidence of life in the form of seeds and microscopic animals. After the Mount Saint Helens eruption, fireweed *(right)* was one of the first plants to appear, scattering its feathery seeds on the wind. Ten years later, small spruce trees began to sprout among the trunks of trees killed in the eruption *(below)*.

Colonizing an Island

How do plants and animals colonize isolated islands? Some seeds and insects arrive by air, either carried for long distances by the wind or stuck to the beaks, feet, feathers, or droppings of birds. Other settlers come by sea. The coconut *(left)* can survive for months floating on ocean currents before washing up on a new beach and sprouting. Animals such as lizards, mice, and snails may arrive on pieces of driftwood, tangles of roots, or other debris.

Earth Churners

After the eruption of Mount Saint Helens, animals like these elk helped speed the recovery. They broke up the crusty volcanic ash with their hoofs, exposing soil. Seeds transported in their droppings and stuck to their fur helped create thriving pockets of vegetation, recolonizing an otherwise barren landscape.

Finding New Species

You may think that by now nearly all the plants and animals in the world would have been discovered. In fact, we are nowhere near a complete count of all the living things on this planet. About 1.75 million **species** of plants and animals have been labeled, but scientists estimate that between three million and 100 million more have yet to be identified.

The biologists who specialize in naming and categorizing plants and animals are called taxonomists. Each year they identify about 13,000 more species. Most of the life forms left to be named are small organisms living in **habitats** that are hard to see, such as the tops of trees in the rain forest. But scientists continue to find relatively large and previously unknown reptiles and mammals, including marsupials, rodents, bats, monkeys, and deer.

In 1996, scientists got their first glimpse of the world's second-smallest monkey, the dwarf marmoset. Its body is only 15 cm (6 in.) long, and it sports a 23-cm (9-in.) tail. The tiny monkey was discovered in Brazil, home to more than a quarter of all living primates. Since 1990, 11 new monkey species have been found there.

I Was There!

Alan Rabinowitz, an American field biologist for the Wildlife Conservation Society's Asia program, had been working for seven years in Vietnam, Laos, and Cambodia before he heard rumors of the discovery of a new species—the saola, a relative of the buffalo and the spiral-horned antelope *(below, right)*. In 1993 he described his first encounter with the new species in Laos as follows:

"Standing outside the cage, my face pressed against the bars, I was awed by this first adult saola to be viewed outside its mountain habitat. She looked in my direction, then stood and ambled over. Pressing her forehead against mine, she pushed outward, testing bone against bone, then lifted her head and touched my face with her extraordinarily long tongue. Only once before had I experienced such gentleness in a large wild mammal, when I approached a newly captured Sumatran rhino in Borneo."

Saola

In 1992, two biologists noticed unusual horns hanging in a home in a remote village of Vietnam. With the help of local villagers, they found the first living specimen of the previously unidentified saola.

Discovery in New Guinea

Australian mammalogist Tim Flannery experienced the highlight of his career when he came across a fluffy black-and-white mammal in New Guinea in 1994. The creature, which he named Dingiso, is a kind of marsupial called a tree kangaroo. Unlike other tree kangaroos, Dingiso lives mostly on the ground. It's also unusual because of its markings: a white star on its forehead, white bars on its muzzle, and a white belly. Some local people hunt it, but others revere it as an ancestor. Flannery describes his discovery of Dingiso and other new species in a book called *Throwim Way Leg,* an expression in the New Guinea pidgin language that means "to go on a journey."

Mysterious Turtle

In 1963, an Australian scientist noticed turtle hatchlings he had never seen before being sold in pet shops in Sydney. For almost 30 years he searched for the animal in the wild, finding it in 1990. The elusive Mary River creature may be not just a new species but also part of a new **genus.**

People — Edward O. Wilson

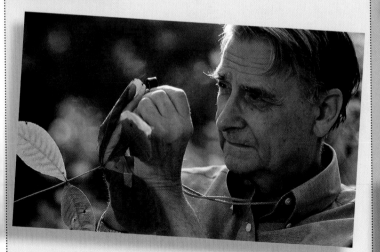

Biologist Edward O. Wilson appreciates the little things in life—like ants. In more than 50 years of research, Wilson has discovered about 300 new ant species. His study of these insects has helped us understand other social animals, including bees and humans.

Strange But TRUE!

Lobster Lips

Scientists in Denmark have discovered a strange new creature in a very weird place—on the lips of Norway lobsters. The microscopic animal feeds by sweeping the lobster's leftovers into its own mouth with hairlike fibers. Even more curious is the way the creature reproduces. Sometimes it mates with another of its kind, but more often it forms buds that break off and grow into adults.

What Can You Do?

It's hard to imagine one person making a difference in the fate of the rain forests or helping to save an endangered **species.** We sometimes forget that when one person does something to help the **environment,** it often triggers a chain reaction, teaching and inspiring others to find ways to protect our world.

Even small changes can make a difference. Whether you decide to address a problem in your hometown or halfway around the world, you can do many things to help protect the earth's precious **natural resources.** A good place to start is with the three R's: reduce, reuse, and **recycle.** Reduce the amount of waste you create. Reuse products as much as possible. Recycle the things you can't reuse, whenever possible.

Plant a Tree

Have you ever thought about all the things trees do for us? They clean the air by absorbing **carbon dioxide** and releasing **oxygen.** They provide fruits and nuts for people and animals to eat. They are a source of paper and lumber. They provide cool shade. And trees are homes for all kinds of wild creatures. You can help keep the world full of trees by planting one in your yard, at your school, or in a community area. You might start a trend that inspires others to plant trees, too.

10 Simple Things

1. Take your lunch to school in a reusable cloth bag instead of a paper or plastic bag.

2. Turn off the water while you brush your teeth.

3. Don't throw food, even apple cores, out the car window. It teaches animals to hunt by the road, where they may be hit by a car.

4. Avoid anything made of Styrofoam. It never decomposes.

5. Write on both sides of a piece of paper.

6. Don't litter—ever.

7. If you don't really need a paper or plastic bag in the checkout line at the store, say so.

8. Snip apart plastic rings on six-packs of soda cans to make sure birds do not get entangled *(above).*

9. Grow a plant in your room to help keep the air clean.

10. Turn off the lights, television, radio, and other appliances when you leave a room.

Recycle

We can all learn a lesson from Will Vinson. When he was nine years old, Will started a recycling program in his hometown of Gainesville, Florida. With the help of his friends and his school's Scout troops, Will raised more than $100 by recycling aluminum cans. He gave the money to the Head Start preschool program.

In Her Own Backyard

In 1972, Jennifer Owen, a naturalist in England, started counting the plant and animal species in her backyard. Since then, in her typical, medium-size town garden she's found nearly 3,000 different species. Most are insects. In the first 11 years, she discovered 13 wasps that had never been found in Britain before. Two were unknown species!

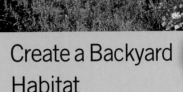

Create a Backyard Habitat

Try it!

You don't need to plant a **forest** to provide a home for plants and animals. You can create a **habitat** in your own backyard. In deciding what to plant, keep in mind that wild animals need food, water, shelter, and a place to raise their young. Plants that produce fruits, nuts, or seeds are a good choice for birds and squirrels. So is dense shrubbery, which will protect them. Don't forget a source of water, such as a birdbath. You could also build a birdhouse or a butterfly hibernation box *(above)*, which mimics the natural crevices where butterflies hide in winter.

Cleaning Up Our Waterways

Rivers, lakes, and ocean shorelines littered with trash are not only ugly to look at, they are also unsafe to use. Many communities near waterways now organize annual events, such as the Anacostia River cleanup day in Washington, D.C. *(below)*.

Volunteers often collect tons of trash. Plastic is the most common litter, but they find all kinds of things from cans and bottles to tires, furniture, and appliances. If your area has a cleanup day, why don't you volunteer to help? If there is no organized event, start one yourself through your school or neighborhood.

Adopt a Cause

Organizations like the Center for Ecosystem Survival sponsor efforts to protect threatened animals and habitats around the world. Their Conservation Parking Meters, found in aquariums, zoos, botanical gardens, and some stores, collect change to help buy and **preserve** unspoiled land around the world. In addition, many zoos offer Adopt an Animal programs so you can contribute directly to the care of an **endangered** species.

Picture Credits

Cover: Book spine, CORBIS/George Lepp; front, art by Jerry Lofaro (background); CORBIS/Craig Aurness; © Sean Morris/Oxford Scientific Films—Reuters/David Loh/Archive Photos.

3: © Michio Hoshino/Minden Pictures. **4:** Peter Velensky/Planet Earth Pictures, London—art by Stephen R. Wagner, © 1997 Time Life Inc.; Jeff Foot Productions—© Tim Flach/Tony Stone Images. **5:** © François Gohier/Photo Researchers Inc.—CORBIS/Gary Braasch; George Grall/National Aquarium, Baltimore. **6, 7:** Butterfly Alphabet/© Kjell Sandved; © 1999 David Muench. **8, 9:** Art by Maria DiLeo; art by Sally Bensusen; CORBIS/Ric Ergenbright; CORBIS/Adam Woolfitt; © Horner/The Hutchison Library, London. **10:** Art by Maria DiLeo; CORBIS/George Lepp. **11:** CORBIS/Craig Aurness; art by Maria DiLeo—CORBIS/Kit Kittle; © Dwight R. Kuhn. **12:** CORBIS/Wolfgang Kaehler; Michelle Burgess/Stock Boston Inc./PNI—© Shin Yoshino/Minden Pictures—© Daryl Balfour/NHPA, Ardingly, Sussex, England. **13:** © Frans Lanting/Minden Pictures; CORBIS/Paul Funston/ABPL. **14, 15:** CORBIS/The Purcell Team; © 1999 Frans Lanting/Minden Pictures—art by Maria DiLeo; Heather Angel, Farnham, Surrey, England; CORBIS/Perry Conway; The Granger Collection, New York. **16:** CORBIS/Galen Rowell; © Fabio Liverani/BBC, NHU Picture Library, Bristol, Avon, England (2)—© Rico & Ruiz/BBC, NHU Picture Library, Bristol, Avon, England. **17:** © 1999 Frank Oberle; © Mitsuaki Iwago/Minden Pictures; CORBIS/Joe McDonald; © Sean Morris/Oxford Scientific Films—CORBIS/George Lepp; © Michio Hoshino/Minden Pictures; CORBIS/Frank Young/Papilio—illustration by Ngaire Sales from *The Nature Company Guide: Walkers Companion*, Weldon Owen Pty. Ltd.; art by Maria DiLeo. **18:** CORBIS/Brent Bear; Tom Nebbia/Schapowalow, Hamburg—© Michael & Patricia Fogden, Bristol, Avon, England—© Art Wolfe/Tony Stone Images. **19:** © Mitsuaki Iwago/Minden Pictures; © Daniel J. Cox/naturalexposures.com—© Frans Lanting/Minden Pictures. **20:** © Michael Quinton/Minden Pictures—CORBIS/Bob Krist. **21:** © Konrad White/Minden Pictures—CORBIS/Anthony Bannister—CORBIS/Frank Blackburn/Ecoscene; © 1993 Frans Lanting/Minden Pictures—CORBIS/Fritz Polking/Frank Lane Picture Agency. **22:** CORBIS/Staffan Widstrand—© 1993 Tim Fitzharris/Minden Pictures; CORBIS/Jim Zuckerman. **23:** CORBIS/Q. Alamany & E. Vicens—Andromeda Oxford Limited, Abingdon, Oxfordshire, England (4); The Granger Collection, New York; Dale M. Brown—© 1999 The Trustees of the National Museums of Scotland. **24, 25:** NASA, image no. 69-HC-199; Rob Wood/Wood Ronsaville Harlin, Inc., © 1997 Time Life Inc.—from *The Nature Company Guide: Weather*, Weldon Owen Pty. Ltd.; Robert M. Carey/NOAA—art by Stephen R. Wagner, © 1997 Time Life Inc. (2); Paul Q. Fuqua (2); © Shin Yoshino/Minden Pictures (2). **26, 27:** Dale M. Brown; map by John Drummond (inset); British Antarctic Survey, Cambridge, Cambridgeshire, England—CORBIS/Jim Zuckerman—© Museum of London (bottom, far left); © 1999 Joanna Pinneo/Aurora; Robert M. Carey/NOAA—John Watson; NASA, image no. 82HC-714. **28, 29:** From *Understanding Science & Nature: Weather & Climate*, Gakken Co., Ltd., Tokyo, 1990; © Nicholas DeVore III/Bruce Coleman, Inc.; Roine Magnusson/Tony Stone Images—© D. Puleston/Photo Researchers Inc.—G. J. Boer & Gregory M. Flato,

Canadian Center for Climate Modeling and Analysis, Atmospheric Environment Service, Victoria, British Columbia, Canada; NASA/Ames Research Center, Moffett Field, Calif. **30:** Map by John Drummond; © Carr Clifton/Minden Pictures—CORBIS/Pat O'Hara—Library of Congress, neg. no. LC-USZ62-8672. **31:** CORBIS/Michael & Patricia Fogden; François Gohier/Photo Researchers Inc. (inset). **32, 33:** CORBIS/Kennan Ward; © Joel Berger (inset); © J. Koivula/Science Source/Photo Researchers Inc.—CORBIS/Tom Brakefield; Paul Q. Fuqua; CORBIS/Pat O'Hara; © Theo Allofs. **34:** CORBIS/Raymond Gehman; © Michael Gadomski/Earth Scenes. **35:** © Carr Clifton/Minden Pictures—Mike McMillan, www.bsstech.com/spotfireimages; art by Maria DiLeo—CORBIS/Jonathan Blair—Giraudon/Paris. **36, 37:** © Tom McHugh/Photo Researchers Inc.; © Ellan Young/Photo Researchers Inc. (background); © James Dickinson/Photo Researchers Inc.; CORBIS/Joe McDonald (2); CORBIS/Wolfgang Kaehler—CORBIS/D. Robert Franz; CORBIS/George McCarthy; © 1979 Ken Brate/Photo Researchers Inc. **38, 39:** © Ian McAllister/Raincoast; Gerry Ellis/ENP Images; © Mark Moffett/Minden Pictures—© Gerry Ellis/Minden Pictures—CORBIS/Raymond Gehman; © Archive Photos—CORBIS/Gary Braasch. **40:** © Art Wolfe; © Mark Moffett/Minden Pictures (2). **41:** © Frans Lanting/Minden Pictures (2)—Mark A. Philbrick/BYU photographer; © Mike Yamashita/Woodfin Camp; © Tim Flach/Tony Stone Images. **42:** CORBIS/Nik Wheeler; © 1993 North Wind Pictures—CORBIS/Charles O'Rear; CORBIS/Nigel J. Dennis/ABPL; CORBIS/Christine Osborne; Günter Ziesler/Bruce Coleman Collection, Uxbridge, Middlesex, England. **44, 45:** Map by John Drummond—© Frans Lanting/Minden Pictures; © 1999 Frank Oberle; CORBIS/Joe McDonald—Paul Q. Fuqua—© 1999 Frank Oberle—Reinhard-Tierfoto/Hans Reinhard, Heiligkreuzsteinach, Germany. **46, 47:** John Dawson/National Geographic Society (NGS) Image Collection—© 1988 David Stoecklein/The Stock Market; © 1995 Frank Oberle; Paul Q. Fuqua; CORBIS/Joe McDonald. **48, 49:** CORBIS/Joe McDonald; Trevor Barrett/Wildlife, Hamburg (inset); © Uwe Walz, Wohltorf, Germany—© Bildarchiv Okapia, Frankfurt; Art Wolfe/Tony Stone Images; Hans-Jurgen Burkard/Bilderberg, Hamburg; Chris Sattlberger/Panos Pictures, London. **50:** Stephanie Maze; © Günter Ziesler, Füssen, Germany—François Gohier (2). **51:** Stephanie Maze (background); © Günter Ziesler—© François Gohier—CORBIS/Wayne Lawler. **52:** David H. Ellis—Cynthia Beall/NGS Image Collection; William Bond/NGS Image Collection. **53:** James Burke—R. Maier/Anthony Picture Power, Eurasburg, Germany; © Tom McHugh/Photo Researchers Inc. **54:** Map by John Drummond—John Dawson/NGS Image Collection; © Bates Littlehales/Earth Scenes/Oxford Scientific Films, Long Hanborough, Oxfordshire, England—CORBIS/Uwe Walz. **55:** Colin Pennycuick/Planet Earth Pictures, London. **56, 57:** Jeff Foot Productions; CORBIS/Kevin Fleming—Anup Shah/Planet Earth Pictures, London; © Nik Wheeler; CORBIS/Eric and David Hosking—© Frans Lanting/Minden Pictures; © Henry H. Holdsworth. **58:** R. Doisneau/Rapho; John Heinrich/Zul Picture Library, Hove, East Sussex, England—CORBIS/Raymond Gehman—Jean-Paul Ferrero/AUSCAPE—Theo Allofs. **59:** John Morgan Photography; Jeffrey W. Lang, 1980/Photo Researchers Inc. (inset). **60, 61:** CORBIS/Phil Schermeister; © Geoff du Feu/Planet Earth Pictures, London; Gary Meszaros—Mark Mattock/Planet Earth Pictures, London—Robert Canis/Planet Earth Pictures, London; E. Doyle Wells, Canadian Forest Service (NRCAN)—CORBIS/Richard Hamilton Smith. **62, 63:** Perry Thorsvik/*Baltimore Sun;* Schapowalow/Comnet, Hamburg;

Glossary of Terms

Acid rain (a-sihd rayn) Rainwater that contains concentrations of acid-forming, or sour, chemicals.

Aerosol (air-oh-sol) **can** A can that sprays a liquid, such as paint or hair spray, that has been packed under pressure with a gas.

Algae (al-jee) A group of simple plants that have no true roots, stems, or leaves.

Alkaline (al-keh-lehn) Having the properties of a salt.

Aquatic (a-**kwa**-tic) Growing in or living in or on the water.

Arid (ay-rid) Dry.

Bacteria (bak-**teer**-ee-uh) A class of microscopic, one-celled, or noncellular organisms.

Biodiversity (bye-oh-dee-**ver**-si-tee) A variety of living organisms.

Biome (bye-ohm) One of the major types of plant and animal communities determined by its climate and geography. Earth has eight major biomes: savanna, grassland, desert, temperate rain forest, deciduous forest, coniferous forest, tundra, and polar region.

Bromeliad (bro-**mee**-lee-ad) A type of plant that lives on another plant and gets its nutrients from rain and air.

Browser (browz-er) An animal that feeds on leaves, young shoots, and twigs, rather than on grass.

Camouflage (kam-uh-flazh) Protective coloring of an organism that lets it blend in with its surroundings, reducing its chances of being detected by its predators or prey.

Carbohydrate (kar-boh-**hye**-drayt) A large group of substances, including sugars and starches, produced by green plants and making up a major food group.

Carbon dioxide (kar-bohn dye-**ox**-eyed) A gas that is used by plants for photosynthesis and exhaled by animals. It forms when fuels containing carbon, such as fossil fuels, are burned.

Cold-blooded (kold-bluhd-id) Lacking the ability to regulate body temperature. The body temperature of a cold-blooded animal fluctuates with the surrounding air or water.

Commensalism (kom-**men**-sah-lism) A relationship between two different types of organisms in which one benefits and the other is not affected.

Community (kuh-**myoo**-nuh-tee) A group of organisms, living in the same area, of different species.

Conservation (kon-ser-**vay**-shun) Preservation from damage or loss.

Conserve (kon-**serv**) To protect from harm or use carefully to avoid waste.

Corrosive (kor-**roh**-suv) Capable of causing a material to dissolve or wear away.

Deciduous (duh-**sihd**-yoo-uhss) Having leaves that turn color and are shed every fall.

Ecosystem (ee-koh-siss-tuhm) The interactions among living and nonliving things in an area, including soil, water, climate, plants, and animals.

Embryo (em-bree-oh) An organism that is in its early stages of development.

Emissions (ee-**mi**-shuns) Matter that is released into the air.

Endangered (en-**dayn**-jurd) In danger of becoming extinct.

Environment (en-**vye**-ruhn-muhnt) The climate, soil, and living things with which an organism interacts and which determine its form and survival.

Equator (ee-**kway**-tur) An imaginary line around the earth, halfway between the North and South Poles.

Erosion (verb, **erode**) (i-**roh**-shuhn, i-**rode**) The breaking down of rock or soil by water, ice, or temperature changes and movement of the particles by water, ice, wind, or gravity.

Evolution (eh-voh-**loo**-shun) The process by which a group of organisms changes over time.

Extinct (ek-**stingkt**) A species that is no longer living.

Famine (fah-min) A prolonged, widespread shortage of food.

Fertile (fur-tul) Able to support plant life or reproduce.

Fertilizer (fur-tuh-ly-zer) A chemical or natural material added to soil that helps plants to grow.

Fluctuate (fluk-choo-ayt) To change continually.

Forest (for-ist) A large area covered with trees and underbrush.

Fossil fuel (foss-sul **fyoo**-uhl) Coal, oil, or natural gas. These fuels are the fossil remains of age-old plants and animals.

Gene (jeen) The basic unit of inheritance.

Gene pool (jeen pool) The genes in an interbreeding population.

Genus (jee-nuhss) A category of biological classification. A genus is composed of species that are structurally related.

Glacier (glay-shur) A large mass of ice that survives for many years where snow accumulates faster than it melts.

Ground water (grownd wa-tuhr) Water that accumulates beneath the earth's surface and supplies springs and wells.

Habitat (hab-i-tat) The natural environment in which a plant or animal lives.

Host (hohst) A plant or animal on which a parasite lives and feeds.

Hot springs A stream of hot water that flows naturally out of the earth.

Individual (in-dee-**vid**-joo-al) A single organism; the basic unit of an ecosystem.

Invertebrate (in-**vur**-tuh-brate) An animal that lacks a backbone or spinal column.

Irrigate (**eer**-ree-gayt) To supply with water through artificial means such as pipes or ditches.

Landfill A waste-disposal system in which an area of land is used to bury garbage and trash under layers of earth.

Marine (**muh**-reen) Living or found in the ocean.

Microorganism (mye-kroh-**or**-guh-niz-uhm) An organism that can be seen only with a microscope.

Mutualism (**myoo**-choo-al-ism) A relationship between two different types of organisms in which both benefit.

Natural resource (**nat**-chur-uhl **ree**-sorss) Anything that can be used by people that is provided by the natural environment, such as trees, minerals, and petroleum.

Natural selection (**nat**-chur-uhl seh-**lec**-shun) The process by which organisms with certain traits survive in a given environment and produce more offspring than do organisms with less-favorable ones.

Niche (nitch) The role played by a species in its ecosystem, including its habitat, feeding activity, interactions with other species, and effects on its surroundings.

Nuclear energy (**noo**-clee-ur **en**-ur-jee) Energy produced by nuclear reactions that generates heat used to produce electricity.

Nutrient (**noo**-tree-uhnt) Microscopic substance used by cells for energy, growth, and repair.

Outback The hot and dry interior of Australia, which is largely uninhabited.

Oxygen (**ok**-suh-juhn) A gas without odor, color, or taste that forms about one-fifth of the air and is necessary for the survival of animals and plants.

Ozone (**oh**-zohn) A form of oxygen containing three oxygen atoms.

Pampas (**pom**-puhs) Extensive grasslands of South America.

Parasite (**payr**-uh-syte) An organism that lives in or on another (the host) and obtains food from it, usually harming and sometimes killing it.

Pesticide (**pess**-teh-syde) A chemical used to kill unwanted plants or animals, such as insects.

Poacher (**poh**-chur) Someone who hunts or fishes illegally.

Pollutant (po-**loo**-tant) Something that harms the environment, making it less suitable for living organisms.

Population (poh-pyoo-**lay**-shun) A group of animals of the same species living in an area.

Precipitation (pri-sip-i-**tay**-shuhn) The forms of water that fall to the ground from the atmosphere: mist, rain, sleet, hail, and snow.

Predator (**pred**-uh-tor) An animal that kills and eats others.

Preserve (**preh**-zerv) To maintain or protect from injury.

Prey (**pray**) An animal hunted or caught for food.

Primate (**prye**-mayt) A group of animals with grasping hands and flexible feet including humans, apes, and monkeys.

Radiation (ray-dee-**ay**-shun) Energy given off in the form of waves or particles.

Radioactive (ray-dee-oh-**ak**-tiv) The giving off of energy and particles by an atom's nucleus.

Recycle (re-**sy**-kel) To reuse or remove useful material from used goods.

Sanctuary (**sank**-choo-ayr-ee) An area where plants and animals are protected.

Saturate (**sa**-chur-ayt) To fill a material full of a liquid.

Savanna (suh-**van**-uh) Tropical grassland with scattered trees and a long dry period alternating with a short wet season.

Sewage (**soo**-ej) Liquid and solid wastes carried off by sewers—underground pipes.

Smog Fog polluted by smoke or chemical fumes.

Soda A salt containing the element sodium.

Species (**spee**-sees) The most specific category of biological classification. A species includes organisms that are similar and can breed only among themselves.

Spring A stream of water that naturally flows out of the earth.

Staple (**stay**-puhl) A basic item of food.

Steppes (steps) Dry, temperate grasslands of southeastern Europe and Asia.

Subtropical (sub-**trah**-pee-kal) Region bordering on the tropics.

Symbiosis (sim-bee-**oh**-suhss) Close association between two organisms that often benefits each of them.

Temperate (**tem**-puh-ruht) An area of mild climate.

Thermophile (**thu**r-meh-fyl) An organism that grows at a high temperature.

Toxic (**tahk**-sik) Poisonous or unhealthy.

Tropic (**trah**-pik) The region north and south of the equator.

Tundra (**tuhn**-druh) A treeless plain with low vegetation that is found mainly in Arctic and sub-Arctic areas with permanently frozen subsoil.

Ultraviolet radiation (uhl-truh-**vye**-oh-let ray-dee-**aye**-shun) A form of high-energy radiation.

Undergrowth (**uhn**-dur-grohth) Plants and shrubs that grow below the trees of a forest.

Updraft A rising current of air.

Urban (**er**-ban) Relating to a city.

Index

Index

Time-Life Education, Inc. is a division of Time Life Inc.

TIME LIFE INC.

PRESIDENT and CEO: Jim Nelson
CHIEF OPERATING OFFICER: Mary Davis Holt

TIME-LIFE EDUCATION, INC.
PRESIDENT: Mary Davis Holt

Time-Life Student Library
OUR ENVIRONMENT

EDITOR: Karin Kinney

Text Editor: Allan Fallow
Associate Editor/Research and Writing: Lisa Krause
Picture Associate: Elizabeth Cook Thompson
Picture Coordinator: Daryl Beard

Designed by: Maria DiLeo, 311 Group

Special Contributors: Mark Galan, Jocelyn Lindsay, Jim Lynch, Jane Martin,
Terrell Smith, Barry Wolverton; Barbara Klein (index)
Senior Copyeditor: Judith Klein
Correspondents: Maria Vincenza Aloisi (Paris), Christine Hinze (London),
Angelika Lemmer (Bonn), Christina Lieberman (New York)

Senior Vice President and Publisher: Rosalyn McPherson Perkins
Sales Director and Associate Publisher: Cheryl Crowell
Vice President of Marketing and Promotion: David Singleton
Director of Book Production: Patricia Pascale
Director of Publishing Technology: Betsi McGrath
Director of Photography and Research: John Conrad Weiser
Production Manager: Vanessa Hunnibell
Director of Quality Assurance: James King
Chief Librarian: Louise D. Forstall

Consultant:

Tim Beach, Ph.D., is associate professor of geography and environmental science
in Georgetown University's program in Science, Technology, and International Affairs
in the School of Foreign Service and director of the Center for the Environment,
Georgetown University. His research investigates the relationships between the
soils-geomorphic environment and people in the Corn Belt of the United States,
the Yucatán of Mexico, Belize, Guatemala, Syria, and Turkey. He teaches courses
on the environmental sciences (climatology, hydrology, geomorphology, and
environmental management) and how these relate to environmental management
and policy.

Library of Congress Cataloging-in-Publication Data
Our environment
    p. cm. — (Time-Life student library)
    Includes index.
    Summary: Describes the world's diverse habitats and the close relationships between
plants and animals, including humans, who must share those habitats.
    ISBN 0-7835-1358-5
    1. Habitat (Ecology)—Juvenile literature. 2. Nature conservation—Juvenile literature.
3. Ecology—Juvenile literature. [1. Habitat (Ecology). 2. Ecology.] I. Time-Life Books.
II. Series.
QH541.14.O87 1999
577—dc21
                                        99-056070
                                          CIP

10 9 8 7 6 5 4 3 2

OTHER PUBLICATIONS

TIME-LIFE KIDS	SCIENCE/NATURE
Library of First Questions and	Voyage Through the Universe
Answers	
A Child's First Library of Learning	DO IT YOURSELF
I Love Math	Custom Woodworking
Nature Company Discoveries	Golf Digest Total Golf
Understanding Science & Nature	How to Fix It
	The Time-Life Complete Gardener
HISTORY	Home Repair and Improvement
Our American Century	The Art of Woodworking
World War II	
What Life Was Like	COOKING
The American Story	Weight Watchers® Smart Choice
Voices of the Civil War	Recipe Collection
The American Indians	Great Taste-Low Fat
Lost Civilizations	Williams-Sonoma Kitchen Library
Mysteries of the Unknown	
Time Frame	
The Civil War	
Cultural Atlas	

For information on and a full description of any of the Time-Life Books series
listed above, please call 1-800-621-7026 or write:

Reader Information
Time-Life Customer Service
P.O. Box C-32068
Richmond, Virginia 23261-2068